Good Musician

The biggest glossary of all music production words, acoustics terms, EDM genres, audio engineering terminology, recording vocabulary, DJ slang, and electronic music theory definitions.

Shadow Producers

Contents

Introduction

Greetings to all musicians, my name is Dan and I have been producing electronic music for more than five years. I am the founder of "Shadow Producers." What exactly does this mean? Shadow Producers is a worldwide team of music producers, music teachers, sound engineers, musicians, DJs and beat makers. Together, we created for you a truly unique product that includes every single word and term (even rare and unique) that you need to know in the world of music creation. The book is suitable both for beginners in music production and audio engineering, and for more professional producers. We hope that you will like this glossary.

Have a great time.

A-B is the procedure for comparing the sound of two separate audio sources, by first listening to one source (A) and then switching to the second (B).

Absolute Phase is a perfect polarity between an original signal (into the microphone) and the reproduced signal (through the speaker).

Absorption, in acoustics, is the process of sound waves absorption by the surface. For example, absorptive materials in the control room tend to "drown out" the sound of the room, because the sound energy is absorbed, rather than reflected.

A cappella: Vocal music without instrumental accompaniment. It contrasts with cantata, which is usually accompanied singing.

Accelerometer is a device that measures the acceleration to which it's subjected and creates a corresponding electrical signal. In music and audio, accelerometers are in such things as guitar pickups and microphones.

Accompaniment is a vocal or instrumental part that supports and enhances another musical part, often a solo.

Acid House can be described as a mix of house music elements with heavy music and bass parts, played on the certain type of synthesizer (Roland TB-303). This genre was developed around the mid-1980s by DJs from Chicago, but the influence of acid house can be heard on later styles of dance music including trance, breakbeat hardcore, jungle, big beat, techno and trip hop.

Acorn Tube is a little vacuum tube, used in ultra-high frequency (UHF) electronics, such as tube amplifiers.

Acoustic Amplifier is a part of some musical instrument (or another device) that vibrates in answer to the first vibration of the instrument, causing the surrounding air to move more efficiently and making the sound louder.

Acoustic Echo Chamber is a room that designed with hard, non-parallel surfaces to create reverberation. In recording studios, they are used to add natural reverb to the dry signal.

Acoustic Engineering is a branch of engineering that deals with sounds and vibrations. Acoustic engineers may apply fundamental scientific principles to find ways to monitor and manipulate sound levels or improve sound clarity. Depending on their area of interest, acoustic engineers may specialize in noise control, architectural acoustics, structural acoustics or underwater acoustics.

Acoustics is a science of the behavior and properties of sound waves. A good understanding of acoustics is significant in the world of music production, audio engineering, and studio design.

Acoustic Shadow is the area, in which sound waves are significantly reduced due obstructions, such as walls, or disruptions, such as wind currents.

Active Device is a component that designed with the ability to control electrical current (as opposed to a Passive Device). Amplifiers in the recording studio are great examples of Active Devices.

Actuator is a part of a switch that causes a change of the contact connections (toggle, pushbutton, rocker, etc.).

ADPCM (Adaptive Delta Pulse Code Modulation) is a method used to convert analog signals to binary signals. The technique converts the analog signals by taking frequent samples of the sound and representing the value of the sampled modulation in binary form. The ADPCM technique is employed to send sound signals through fiber-optic long-distance lines. This is useful especially for organizations that set up digital lines between remote sites to broadcast both voice and data. The voice signals are digitized before they are broadcasted. In the telecommunication field, the ADPCM technique is used mainly in speech compression because the method makes it possible to reduce bit flow without compromising quality. The ADPCM method can be applied to all wave forms, high-quality audio, images and other modern data.

ADSR (abbreviation for "Attack, Decay, Sustain, and Release") means four sections of a sound's envelope that describe the shape of sound over time.

Attack means the point, where the sound begins and increases in volume to its peak.

Decay is the decreasing in volume (to the sustain level), after reaching its peak in the attack stage.

Sustain is the time, during which it stays at this level. In other words, it is the part of the sound that holds at approximately the same volume, after the initial attack, and drops in volume level (decay) until the sound stops playing.

Release is the time it takes for sound to step from the sustain to its final level.

After-Fade Listen (AFL) is a mixing consoles channel function, which allows users to hear an incoming signal after the volume fader, without hearing any other channels.

Aftertouch is a feature on some keyboard instruments, by which applying extra pressure to a key after it has been pressed, may activate an additional MIDI control command.

AIFF is a full resolution digital audio format, initially developed by Apple. It can be stereo or mono, at sampling rates up to 48 kHz.

Aliasing can mean:
1) The effect that causes various signals to become indistinguishable (or aliases of one another) when sampled;
2) An undesired frequencies that are arisen when harmonic components within the audio signal being generated by a digital sound source, or sampled by a digital recording device, lie above the Nyquist frequency. Aliasing differs from any other types of noise in that its pitch changes significantly when the pitch of the intended sound changes.

Altered Chord is a chord, in which one or more tones have been changed from its normal pitch in the key.

Ambience, in recording, refers to the part of the sound that comes from the surrounding environment, rather than directly from the sound source. For example, any sound waves, coming into your ears from any music instruments, are coming directly from the source, but the sounds of the same instruments, coming to you after bouncing off the back wall, are ambient sounds.

Ambient Field is the area away from the sound source, where the reverberation is louder than the main sound.

Ambient House is a subgenre of house music that combined elements of ambient music and acid house. Ambient house first emerged in the late 1980s. Tracks in this genre, typically, feature four-on-the-floor beat patterns, synth pads, and vocal samples integrated into a style, classed as "atmospheric."

Ambient Music is a genre of electronic music that puts an emphasis on tone and atmosphere over traditional musical structure and rhythm. Ambient music is said to evoke a "visual," "atmospheric," or "unobtrusive" quality.

Amplifier is a device that increases the level or amplitude of an electrical signal, making the sound louder.

Amplitude is the height of a waveform below or above zero line. In audio, it refers to the signal strength or the volume of the sound.

Amplitude Modulation (AM) means a multiplication of one time-domain signal by another time-domain signal. That signals may be electrical in nature, or vibration signals, and they also may contain harmonics components. AM is a non-linear process and always gives rise to frequency components that did not exist in either of the two original signals.

Analog Recording means a recording of the continuous changes of an audio waveform. Analog recording methods store signals as a continuous signal in or on the media. The signal may be stored as a physical texture on a phonograph record, or a fluctuation in the field strength of a magnetic recording. This is different from digital recording where digital signals are quantized and represented as discrete numbers.

The most typical example of analog recording is recording on reel-to-reel magnetic tape.

Arp (abbreviation to "Arpeggio") refers to playing individual notes of chord one after another, rather than all at once.

Arranging, in electronic music, is the process of transforming a collection of musical ideas, separately recorded instruments, and different parts of a song into a complete track; selection of instruments playing in each section and how the sections themselves are arranged within the larger timeline of the song.

Artifacts mean undesirable, but audible sounds that arise as side-effects of digital sound processing. In electronic music (especially in glitch music), these artifacts are created specifically to make music from them.

ASIO (Audio Stream Input/Output) is a multi-channel audio transfer protocol that bypasses the normal audio path from a user application through the layers of intermediary Windows operating system software, so that an application connects straight to the sound card hardware.

Atonality refers to the music, in which no tonic or key center is apparent. Atonality usually describes compositions written from about 1907 to the present day, where tonality is not used as a composition foundation.

Attenuation, in audio, means the reduction in volume. Measured in decibels (dB) sound waves traveling through the air, naturally attenuate, as they removed from the source of the sound.

Audio is the range of frequencies that humans can hear. In the technical sense, audio refers to the transmission, recording, or reproduction of the sound.

Auto BPM Counter is a feature, usually on mixers, which calculates and displays the BPM of a tune.

Automatic Gain Control is a compressor with a long release time, which is used to maintain the volume of the audio at the permanent level.

Auto-Tune is an audio processor, which uses a proprietary device to measure and alter pitch in vocal and instrumental music recording. Auto-Tune users set a reference point – a scale or specific notes, for example – and a rate at which derivations from this point will be digitally corrected. This rate can be carefully calibrated so a voice sounds "natural," by tacking the voice smoothly back to the reference pitch. Also, artists can make the correction happen quickly and artificially, which results in the warbling, digitized voices now all the rage in pop, hip-hip, reggae and other types of music.

Nowadays, 90% or more of all "professional" recordings use this software.

Auxiliary Return (Aux Return) is the input on a console or DAW, which returns the affected signal, sent through the auxiliary, and sends it back into the channel mix.

Auxiliary Send (Aux Send) is a control to regulate the signal level being transmitted from the input channel on a DAW or console to auxiliary equipment, or plugins through the auxiliary bus. It is commonly used for creating an effects loop that processes a part of the signal and then returns it into the mix through the auxiliary return.

Axis means an imaginary line, around which a device operates.

Baffles refer to sound absorbing panels that are used to prevent sound waves from entering or leaving a space.

Balance is the relative level of musical instruments in a mix (or audio signals in the channels) of a stereo recording. Balance can also refer to a comparison in tonal quality rather than just volume, such as the contrast between a light or "airy" sounding instrument timbre with a heavy or "dark" sounding timbre. Equalization, achieved by modern equalizers, adjust volumes at specific bandwidths to achieve balance in overall tone.

Balancing Levels is a technique, used to make your music as loud as possible, without making it sound distorted or damaging the speakers.

Band Track is a mixed track, containing only the instrumental parts of the song.

Bandwidth, in signal processing, refers to the usable frequency range of a communication channel, measured by the difference between the device's lowest and highest frequencies.

Banger, in music, is a slang for unbelievably awesome and cool track.

Bank is a group of sound modules as a unit, or a collection of sound patches, sequencer data, or operating parameters of a synthesizer's generators.

Bar is a group of beats. The actual number of beats, contained within the bar, depends on different music styles, but in dance music, a bar usually contains four beats.

Baritone is a type of classical male singing voice, whose vocal range lies between the bass and the tenor voice types. Baritone refers to a tone that is second lowest in pitch within its sonic family. It is the most common male voice. There is also baritone saxophone (between tenor and bass saxophone), baritone guitar (between standard tuning and bass guitar), and so on.

Basic Session means the first audio recording session for recording the basic tracks that serve as the song's foundation.

Bass refers to sound with a very low and deep frequency (16-256 Hz).

Bass Boost is a circuit that emphasizes the lower audio frequencies, generally by attenuating higher audio frequencies.

Bass Reflex Speaker is a type of loudspeaker, designed in such way that back wave of a speaker cone is routed via an open port (sometimes called "a tube" or "vent") in the enclosure, to increase output volume, decrease distortion, and improve bass response and extension.

Beaming is a phenomenon found in loudspeakers, in which higher frequencies are projected directly from the loudspeaker, rather than scattering along with the lower frequencies.

Beat is an even, steady pulse in music. In popular use, beat can refer to a variety of related concepts including: rhythm, tempo, meter, and groove.

Blast Beat is a type of rapid drum beat, characteristic of extreme heavy metal styles. Blast beats are made with rapid alternating or coinciding strokes primarily on the bass and snare drum.

Downbeat is the first beat of a bar.

Upbeat is the last beat in the previous bar, which immediately precedes, and hence anticipates, the downbeat.

Beat Mapping is the process of adjusting the tempo variations in a recorded piece of music, in accordance with a given tempo of the whole project. In DAW, it's done using time-stretching tools and cuts to synchronize transients with the corresponding tempo markers.

Beatmatching is a technique, predominantly used by DJs, to synchronize the tempos of two recorded tracks and create seamless and smooth transition from one song into another.

BGV is an abbreviation for "Background Vocals."

Bi-amplification is a technique, in which high and low frequencies in a speaker driven by two separate amplifiers.

Big Room House is a subgenre of electro house music that began to develop in 2010 and gained popularity through EDM-oriented festivals. The tempo is generally about 126-132 BPM. This genre often incorporates drops, minimalist percussion, regular beats, sub-bass kicks, simple melodies, and voice insert right before the drops.

Bitcrushing is the process of reducing the accuracy of a digital signal. For example, we've got a signal recorded at the audio CD standard 16-bit resolution, by reducing it to an 8-bit resolution we discard some of the information. As a result, the signal becomes less accurate. The more information we discard, the less accurate the signal becomes.

Bit depth is the number of bits of information in each sample. In other words, it is the level of detail in audio file (usually 16 or 24 bit).

Bitpop is a type of electronic music (and subgenre of chiptune), in which at least a part of the music is created using the sound chips of an old 8 or 16-bit computers and video game consoles.

Bitrate means the number of bits, which can be conveyed per second, typically measured in Kbps.

Blending means the mixing of multiple sounds or channels together to form a single sound, or mixing the left and right signals together.

Booth is the area where a DJ, turntables, mixer and other equipment are located at the club.

Bootleg, in general, means objects that are copied and sold illegally. In the music industry, bootleg is something that is used in violation of copyright laws, especially something that is duplicated and sold for profit, when the person selling it has no legal right to copy or sell it.

Bouncing ("Ping-Ponging" or simply "Ponging") is a technique of mixing multiple tracks into one or two tracks (stereo or mono). This method can be done digitally, through a digital audio workstation, in analog form, by playing the tracks on the console and recording them into separate tracks, and in real-time.

Breakdown is a part of a song, in which different instruments have solo parts (breaks). For example, when all instruments play some part of the song together, and then several of them individually repeat these parts solo.

Bridge (or "Break") is usually used in electronic music right before the second drop or chorus to break up and contrast what the audience draws attention to. This section is very short and not repeated over the course of the song. Bridge creates a tension that leads power to the next section.

Bridging is a technique of supplying a single input to both channels of an amplifier and summing them into one, thereby doubling the amplifier power supplied to the signal.

Brightness means the amount of high-frequency signals present in the audio.

Bucking is a type of phase cancellation, in which two frequencies (or signals) with the same amplitude but different polarity, cancel one another out.

Bulk Dump (short for "System Exclusive Bulk Dump") is a method of transmitting data, such as internal parameters between MIDI devices. Basically, it means to send (dump) the contents of a certain part of the memory of the device over the MIDI cables, via some code, known as "SysEx" (system exclusive). The data can be received then by a sequencer (recorded) and utilized in some way, such as by being stored, modified, etc.

Bumper is a small cut of music that can be used to introduce, end or connect various sections of audio or audiovisual production.

Bus means any audio conduit that allows a selection of different signals to be processed (or routed) them together. You supply the desired signals to the bus, use processing to the resulting mixed signal, and then direct the signal to your destination place.

Busk means to perform music in the streets and public places, usually for money.

Bypass is a switch that allows a signal to pass through an effects processor without processing the signal. Depending on the DAW, it may be either a **regular bypass**, in which case a signal passes through the processing circuitry, but the signal is unaffected by the processor, or a **true bypass**, in which case the signal passes directly from the input to the output without passing through the effect's circuitry.

Call and Response is a sequence of two separate phrases, where the second phrase sounds like a direct response to the first phrase. In electronic music, this term refers more to notes, when one note "responds" to another, creating a certain chord.

Cantata means a vocal composition with an instrumental accompaniment.

Capstan is a mechanical part of the tape recorder that controls tape speed as it passes through the tape heads.

Channel is a single path that an audio signal can go through a device, from an input to an output.

Channel Path means the complete signal path from the sound source to the multitrack recorder (or DAW).

Chase is an automatic adjustment of the speed of a recorder (or sequencer) to be time with another recorder.

Chill-out Music ("Chillout," "Chill out," or simply "Chill") is a subgenre of electronic music and collective term for several electronic music styles, characterized by their "soft" sounding and mid-tempo beats. Chill-out music emerged in the early and mid-1990s at dance clubs, where relaxing music was played to give the dancers some chance to "chill out" from the more fast-tempo music, played on the main dance floor.

Chillstep is a musical genre, composed of dubstep tracks with chill undertones. Chillstep offers low bass, slow beats, simple drums, and serene vocals to provide a landscape of sound which has subtle dubstep elements.

Chiptune ("Chip music" or "8-bit music") is synthesized electronic music which is made for programmable sound generator (PSG) sound chips used in vintage computers, consoles, and arcade machines.

Chord refers to two or more (usually three) musical pitches (notes), sung or played together. Chords are built off of a single note, called the **root**. The most frequently played chords are **triads**, a grouping of three notes: the root note, and intervals of a third and a fifth above the root note. If a chord is played with all its tones as close together as they can be, then it's in **close position**. If the notes are spread out then it's in **open position**.

Chord Chart is a shorthand form of musical notation that provides the basic chord changes and essential rhythmic information of a song.

Enharmonic Chords are chords that differing in notation, but similar in sound. Such chords are called "enharmonically changed," and passing from one to the other is an "enharmonic modulation."

Chorus, in popular use, means the main part of the song that repeats with the same music and lyrics every time, often containing the main point of the song and a hook. This part should have a lot of energy and be no longer than the verse. As for the music production,

chorus effect is an effect that doubled and detuned your signal. It is designed to make a signal sound like it was produced by a plenty of similar sources. For example, if you add a chorus effect to the voice of a solo singer, his voice will sound like a chorus. This effect works by adding multiple short delays to the signal, but instead of repeating the same delay, each delay is "variable length." It adds the randomness, needed for the chorus sound. Changing the delay time also varies the pitch slightly, further adding to the "multiple sources" illusion.

Click Track means a single track of audio, which contains some simple ticking sound, or rhythmic clicking (like a metronome), that matches the tempo of a musical performance.

Clock Signal is a signal sent by a device within the circuit that generates steady pulses to keep other devices in sync with each other. In the EDM world, a good example of clock signal is the sequencing through MIDI: the sequencer sends a clock signal so that the connected devices will play in time.

Coda refers to a few measures, added to the end of a piece of music, to "round it off" or make a more powerful ending.

Coffin is a heavy-duty case for carrying DJing equipment. Usually designed to carry two turntables and a mixer in a long shallow case, resembling a coffin. The lid can be entirely removed so that you can use your equipment without having to take it all out.

Collaboration is the process where two or more producers or musicians are working together to produce and release a joint track.

Compander is a signal processor, serving as a combination compressor and expander, primarily used for noise reduction purposes in analog systems.

Companding (is a combination of the words "compressing" and "expanding") refers to a technique for compressing and then expanding (or decompressing) an analog or digital signal. The use of companding allows signals with a large dynamic range to be transmitted over facilities that have a smaller dynamic range capability.

Comping, in digital audio workstations, is the process of blending portions of multiple recorded takes to create a "compilation" track.

Compression is the process of reducing an amplitude range of audio signal by reducing the peaks and bringing up the low levels. Also, compression can mean the process of reducing data file in size (some types of audio compression may reduce the sound quality).

Compression Ratio is the rate by which a compressor attenuates an incoming signal; measured in decibels.

Compressor is a signal processor or plugin that lowers the dynamic range of an audio signal by raising its quieter sections and reducing its louder ones. Compressors work like an automatic volume control, attenuating the volume whenever it rises above a certain level (called "the threshold"). By lowering peak levels, the compressor allows you to increase the overall signal level, which gives the sound a greater focus. Also, compression tends to make sounds tighter or "punchier."

Main types of compression:

Downward Compression refers to the loudness averaging of a sound wave, by reducing the signal level of all sound that is above a particular threshold, while leaving any sounds below the threshold untouched. In other words, it brings the loud noises down closer in relation to the quiet noises, all while leaving the quiet noises unchanged.

Multiband Compression is a type of compression, where a particular frequency band (typically specified by the sound engineer or producer) is compressed, rather than the entirety of the audio signal, as is usually the case with regular compressors. It might be very helpful if you want, for example, to tighten the low mids of a bass sound, without taking away from the high end. Just choose the frequency you want to alter, set the threshold, attack, and release accordingly.

Parallel Compression involves mixing an unprocessed dry signal with a compressed version of the same signal. For example, you can take some part of drum mix, compress it, and after that mix it with the original part. It enables you to maintain the transients of the original signal, but add some "impact" of the compressed signal as well.

Serial Compression involves putting two (typically different) compressors in series. For example, you might use a faster compressor first, followed by a slower one. You get the character of both compressors, and thus you can get such sounds that you would not get with just one compressor.

Sidechain Compression is a form of compression that uses an external audio signal to affect compressed sound. A sidechain compressor uses different signal, other than the primary input, to manage the amount of compression. It is often used in mastering to compress an audio at a particular frequency range, by equalizing the original signal in a separate path and feeding it into the side chain to control the level.

Upward Compression refers to compressing signals below a particular threshold, to bring up some presence energy in a sound. When the sound lacks definition or detail, upward compression is a great way to bring back some of that things.

Conjunct is a stepwise melodic motion, in which the notes of a melody located very close to each other.

Consonance is a combination of notes or sounds, which are in harmony with each other, due to the relationship between their frequencies.

Constant Bitrate is an option of data encoding (including audio), at which the bitrate does not change throughout the entire file.

Control Voltage (CV) is a DC electrical signal, which is used as an analog method of controlling synthesizers, drum machines, and other devices with external sequencers. If you send a particular electrical voltage to a module of an analog synthesizer (such as an ADSR envelope generator), you can indicate what you want this module to do.

Copyright, in music, is a property right, which appears at the moment of creation of a song or sound recording. It gives content creators and owners an exclusive right to make copies, license and otherwise exploits their work. In the music industry, there are copyrights relating to lyrics, music, and the actual sound recording.

Core Audio is a set of services and drivers, used to implement music and audio on Apple's macOS and IOS operating systems. It is similar to ASIO for PCs.

Crisp describes a good, clean sound with a high mid-range.

Critical Distance means a distance from the source of a sound, at which direct sound and reverberant sound are at the same volume level. Critical distance depends on the location; in the reverberation room, the critical distance will be closer to the source and in a room with absorptive walls, the distance will be further from the source.

Cross-correlation is a measure of the similarity of two signals in the time domain. If the signals are identical, the cross correlation will be one, and if they are completely different, the cross correlation will be zero.

Crossfade Looping is a sample-editing feature, found in many sample-editing software and samplers, in which some part of the data at the beginning of a loop is mixed with some part of the data at the end of the same loop, to provide a smoother transition between the beginning and the end of the loop.

Crossfading is a method that creates a smooth transition from one sound to another. This audio effect works similar to the fader, but in different directions, which means that the first source can fade in, while the second fades out, and it all mixes. Crossfading often uses in audio engineering, for blending multiple sounds in the same song and creating a smooth transition among them or to just filling the silence between two tracks.

Crossover is an electrical circuit, consisting of a combination of filters that divides an audio signal into two or more bands or signals, normally to be fed into various components of the loudspeaker system, in accordance with the frequency range.

Active Crossovers split frequency bands prior to amplification of the audio signal.

Passive Crossovers split frequency bands after amplification of the audio signal, just before reaching the individual loudspeaker components.

Crossover Frequency means the frequency, at which the crossover stops sending the signal to one speaker and starts sending it to the other one.

Cross-switching is a velocity threshold effect in the synthesizer, in which one sound is triggered at low velocities and the other at high velocities, with a sharp transition between them.

Crosstalk means unwanted leakage of an audio signal between two audio channels.

Cue is a tool for preparing the next song to be played. In many mixers, "the cue button" allows you to set the point, at which a song will start playing, and after that you need to keep pressing "the cue button" until the beat in your headphones equals the beat that's playing on the speakers.

Cutoff Slope is the rate of decreasing of the frequencies beyond the passband of a filter. In other words, the slope is the number of dB, to which the filter reduces the signal for every octave past the cutoff frequency.

CV/Gate (Control Voltage/Gate) is an analog method of regulating synthesizers, drum machines, and other related equipment with external sequencers. The control voltage, normally, controls pitch and the gate signal controls note on-off.

Daisy Chain means a connection of several devices in such manner that the signal must pass via one device to get to the second device, and via the second device to get to the third device, and so on.

Damping means a dissipation of the vibratory energy in solid structures with distance or time. It's analogous to the absorption of sound in air. Can refer to the diminished amplitude in an electrical signal or the suppressed vibrations of a musical instrument (such as the damper pedal on an acoustic piano).

Viscous Damping means damping that occurs when a particle in oscillating system is resisted by a force that has a value proportional to the magnitude of the velocity of the particle and direction opposite to the direction of the particle.

DAO (Disc at Once) is a recordable CD method, in which the session is recorded in one pass, without any break (the laser doesn't turn off).

Dark Ambient (till the 1980s was called "Ambient Industrial") is a genre of post-industrial music that features ominous, foreboding, or discordant overtones, some of which were massively inspired by elements of ambient music.

DC Offset is an undesirable characteristic of sound recording. It occurs in the capturing of sound before it reaches the recorder. The cause is almost always a fixed voltage offset somewhere in the audio chain before the analog signal is converted to digital values. For example, the voltage may be directly caused by a faulty sound card. Audio editing software often comes with a filter to remove it because it contains no audio information.

Dead Air is an extended period when the band is on stage, but no music is being played nor is anyone talking.

Decibel (abbreviated "dB") is the ratio measurement of two levels according to a scale, where a certain percentage change comprises one unit. Most often used to describe audio levels.

Decompression is the process, in which a data file that has been previously decreased in size using compression is restored to a usable form.

Deep House is a subgenre of house music that originated in the 1980s. Deep house track has a tempo between 120 and 125 BPM and includes elements of jazz and ambient; characterized by an easy but, at the same time, deepened atmospheric sound with a minimum set of instruments.

De-esser is an audio compressor, designed to reduce the volume of sibilant sounds and frequencies, especially those produced by pronouncing the letter "s" (range of sibilants between 2 kHz-10 kHz, depending on the person).

Delay is a process, by which an audio signal is recorded on a device, reproduced at a time delay, and then mixed with the original, non-delayed signal, for creation a variety of effects. **Delay effect** can be used to double individual sounds (as if a group of musical instruments is playing the same melody), to achieve an echo effect (as if this melody was recorded in a vast space), and to improve the stereo positioning of tracks in the mix. Delays are also provided parameters for feedback (called "**regeneration**"), which let you specify how much of the delayed signal will be fed back to the delay's input, creating more delay repetitions (like the amount of "bounces" in an echo).

Grain Delay slices an input audio into very short segments (granules) and then delays each slice by a slightly different time. Most granular delays incorporate pitch-shifters, which allow them to change the pitch of each slice.

Granular delays are the most complex delay plugins and can warp and mangle audio into an entirely different sound.

Group Delay is an aspect of all electronic audio devices (amplifiers, speakers, etc.), in which different frequencies in the signal are output with small delays from one another. In other words, lower frequencies are delivered slightly more slowly than higher ones.

Initial Time Delay (ITD) is the gap in time between the arrival of direct sound and the first sound reflected from a surface.

Long Delay means a delay times above 60 milliseconds.

Multi-tap Delay is a delay effect, where the delay time can be divided into multiple "taps".

For example, you might set the delay for 480 milliseconds, and then have taps at 1/2 that time (240ms) and 1/3 that time (160ms). (Contrast this with a "normal" delay, where you would only be able to get repeats at even intervals, in this example, 120, 240, 360, and 480ms or 160, 320, and 480ms, but not a combination of the two).This allows you to create rhythmic delay effects, based on repeats at 160, 240, and 480 milliseconds.

Ping-pong Delay includes two delay units, one for the left channel of audio and one for the right. By shifting the audio between the two, the plug-in creates a "bouncing" effect, as the sound moves from one channel to another and back.

Pre-delay is a parameter on a reverb unit or a plugin, which defines the amount of time (delay) between the original dry signal and the early reflections of reverberation. This characteristic is usually used to simulate the natural acoustic properties of a room, but can also be used to produce impressive unnatural effects.

Short Delay means a delay times under 20 milliseconds.

Slapback Delays are very short delays, with (usually) just a single tap. These were often used in blues and country guitar tones, and are very evocative of those styles.

Tape Delay is a signal processing technique for creating artificial delay or echoes, by manipulating time delays with analog tape machines. Back in the "old days", producers and engineers created delay and echo effects using tape machines.

Nowadays, most tape delay effects in the recording studio are reproduced digitally through plugins in a DAW.

Demo is a preliminary recording, designed to give the listener an idea of how the song can sound in the final production.

Demodulation means a process of extracting a signal from a carrier wave, upon which the signal was originally imposed during modulation. For example, the process of extracting voice or music from an FM broadcast signal.

Denoise means to eliminate or reduce many kinds of low-level noise from an audio signal.

Detent is a point of slight physical resistance in the travel of a knob or slide control. Most knobs on mixers are detent to indicate their unity gain or centered position.

Detune refers to intentionally lowering or raising the pitch, produced by a musical instrument. This effect can be used for a number of purposes in the studio, but is often used in "double-tracking," blending a detuned track (or instrument) with the original to create fuller sound.

Diffraction is described as the bending of waves around an obstacle. Depending on the size of the object and the wavelength of the sound, the sound wave diffuses around the object and the diffraction or interference is significant. Similarly when sound waves pass through a gap they spread out depending on the wavelength (frequency) and a gap size.

Diffusion is a scattering of sound energy. When sound bounces of hard flat surfaces, the energy remain intact yielding discrete echoes, which degrade speech intelligibility and music clarity (sound diffusers can deal with this problem).

Also, "diffusion" can refer to a parameter found on many reverb units or plug-ins that determines how diffuse the reflections are. A low setting produces reflections (such as distinct echoes), while higher settings produce smeared and indistinct sounds.

Digipack is a type of CD case, which looks like a book, rather than a plastic case. A digipak can flip open like a book or it can have three parts so that one portion of the packaging opens to the right and one to the left with the CD presented in the center portion.

Digital Audio Extraction (or "Ripping") is a method of retrieving audio samples from an audio CD, to create a computer audio file.

Digital Recording is the process of converting audio signals into numbers that represent the waveform, and then storing these numbers as data.

Digital Vinyl System (also known as "DVS") is vinyl emulation software that allows users to physically manage and manipulate the playback of digital audio files on a computer with the help of turntables, as an interface, thereby preserving the hands-on control and sense of DJing with vinyl.

Diminish means to lower by one semitone.

Dipping (or "dip") is the opposite of "peaking" and used in audio to describe the shape of a frequency response curve that looks like a precipice or a dip.

Direct Injection (DI) is the process of sending an electrical audio signal from an instrument directly to the mixing console, through the use of electric pickups or direct boxes.

Direct Out is an output, which is fed directly from the preamplifier stage of the input, bypassing faders and channel strips. This function is often used to send a "dry" signal to a monitor mix or a recording device.

Disjunct is a stepwise melodic motion, in which the notes of a melody located far apart from each other.

Dispersion means a change in the shape of the sound wave (sound pulse) when it scattered in the medium. Each speaker has both a vertical and a horizontal dispersion angle, at which the sound level is a few dB lower than if you were standing directly in front of the speaker.

Dissonance is a definition that refers to a lack of harmony in music. In other words, it is a combination of notes that sound strange because they are not in harmony.

Distortion refers to the deformation of the waveform at the output of the device, compared to the input, usually due to overload, generating a distorted or "dirty" signal. In electronic music, sound distortion is frequently used to create certain audio effects. **Distortion effect** simulates the sound of analog and digital distortion and includes tone parameters that allow you to determine how the distortion changes your signal, and enable you to control on how much distortion increases the output level of the signal.

Amplitude Distortion is a distortion, occurring in a system or a device when the output amplitude is not a linear function of input amplitude.

Clipping is a form of audio distortion, which appears because of overloading an electronic device. Named so because its graphic waveform looks as if the edges of the waveform were "clipped."

Crossover Distortion is a type of distortion, which is caused by switching between devices driving a load. It occurs in push-pull class AB or class B amplifiers, during the time that one side of the output stage shuts off, and the other turns on. Crossover distortion is most thought of as a problem only with low-level signals, but digital converters are also sometimes plagued with this problem (but it is more a manifestation of quantization error at low bit depths).

Frequency Distortion ("Amplitude-Frequency Distortion" or "Waveform-Amplitude Distortion") is a type of distortion, in which the relative magnitudes of the different frequency elements of a wave are changed, during transmission or amplification.

Harmonic Distortion is the presence of harmonics in the output signal of a device, which weren't present in the input signal, ordinarily for the purpose of changing the instrument's timbre.

Intermodulation Distortion is a distortion, caused by two or more audio signals of different frequencies, interacting with one another.

Phase Distortion is a change in the sound, because of a phase shift in the signal. Phase distortion synthesizers are subtractive synthesizers, but with some differences – they use the waveform flexibility of wavetable synthesis in the oscillator, and instead of choosing waves for selection on the oscillator, you are given full control above the shape of the waveform between all set forms.

THD (Total Harmonic Distortion) can be described as a measure of the difference between the harmonic frequency level at the output stage of the amplifier, as compared to the input stage, expressed as a percentage. It's a very fine-tuning specification, hardly perceptible to many ears, but the lower the THD, the more accurately the amplifier (or speaker) plays the sound.

TIM (Transient Intermodulation Distortion) occurs in amplifiers that apply negative feedback when signal delays make the amplifier unable of correcting distortion when exposed to fast, transient signals.

Dithering is an artificial blending of white noise (or other noises) to the audio signal. Dithering adds amplitude to all signals in a digital sample. It forces the lower level amplitude values up to the next threshold level. These new signals with higher amplitude now represent the sum of the dither noise and the previously existing amplitude. The lower level bits are filled in with the dither noise and become the least significant bits (in terms of amplitude) in the 24-bit signal. Then, as the file is cut from 24-bit to 16-bit, only the lower 8 bits is truncated thus leaving behind the previous signal plus some noise.

Diversity, in audio, is the use of two or more antennas in a wireless receiver system to prevent failures in sound.

DJ Mix is a sequence of musical tracks, typically mixed to appear as one continuous track. These mixes are usually performed using a DJ mixer and multiple sounds sources, such as turntables. A DJ mix demands that the tracks be changed and modified in some manner; if the tracks have not been changed, then the action, which should be described by relationships, is a **compilation**, but not DJ mixing.

Downtempo is a genre of electronic music that originated in the late 1980s in the United Kingdom; characterized by a slow rhythm. Downtempo close to trip-hop, but differs from it by a less pressing and depressive musical atmosphere, also sounds similar to ambient music, but with a greater emphasis on rhythm, often consisting of loops with a "hypnotic" effect.

Drone Music is a minimal music genre, which emphasizes the use of sustained or repeated sounds, notes, or tone-clusters – called **drones** (notes or chords, which are sounds throughout most or all of the composition).

Drop is an expression that means the moments in songs, in which music is focused on increasing the intensity of a sound, which is usually accompanied by a large number of bass. Usually, it is the heaviest part of a track and the part, where people on a dance floor are most active.

Dropout is a brief loss of data in a digital audio file, or a brief loss of audio signal on tape, which can result in an unwanted dip and crackle in audio.

Drum and Bass ("drum 'n' bass," "drum & bass," "D&B" or "DnB") is a genre and branch of electronic music that emerged in England, during the early 1990s. The style is often characterized by fast breakbeats (typically 160–180 beats per minute) with heavy bass and sub-bass lines.

Drum Machine is an electronic device, which containing sampled and synthesized drum sounds in its memory, as well as an internal sequencer that can be programmed to play drum loops or patterns.

Drum Pattern is a certain sequence of drum sounds, sequenced by a drum machine or played by a drummer, for use in a song.

DSP (Digital Signal Processing) is any signal processing done after an analog audio signal has been converted into digital audio.

Dubstep is an EDM genre that originated in the late 1990s in South London, England. Dubstep characterized by a tempo of about 140-150 beats per minute, the dominant low-frequency bass with the presence of sound distortion, and also the rarefied breakbeat in the background.

Ducking is a compression-based audio effect, in which an audio signal proportionately reduced by the presence of another audio signal.

Duration is the amount of time, during which the sound is heard. This factor can be controlled via the envelope generator of a synthesized sound.

Duty Cycle is the part of one period, in which a signal is active. Expressed as a percentage or a ratio.

Dynamic Signal Processing (DSP) is the process of automatically changing the relationship level between the loudest audio and the softest audio. Dynamic processors include limiters, compressors, expanders, and gates.

Echo is a reflection of a sound that comes with a delay after the direct sound. We recognize an echo's sounds when the distance between the source and the reflection is far enough from each other so that we can detect the time delay between one and the other. Reverb, for example, is a sort of combination of many echoes, occurring too fast to hear each individually. In the recording studio, echoes can be reproduced acoustically or synthesized by a digital signal processor.

Anechoic means free from echoes and reverberations.

Echo Chamber is an enclosed room, designed with reflective, non-parallel surfaces, which is used to produce reverb sounds, usually for recording purposes.

Flutter Echo is an acoustic effect in some rooms, where a sound is reflected back and forth between two parallel surfaces, such as opposite walls. So the sound gets "trapped" between two surfaces for a while and we get this effect.

Pre-echo (or "Forward echo") is a compression artifact that usually occurs in digital audio, in which an "echo" of a sound is heard ahead of the sound itself, frequently due to the data inconsistencies in some compressed digital formats.

Reverse Echo is a sound effect, produced as the result of recording an echo or delayed signal of an audio recording that played backwards.

Slap Echo (or "Slapback") is a single, clear echo of a sound, which can naturally arise at higher frequencies reflected from the nonabsorbent wall, or simply reproduced by a signal processing unit or plugin. This type of echo creates a "live" sound, similar to what you might have heard in some arena.

Edgy means a sound with harmonics that are too strong relative to the fundamentals, resulting in distorted or a raspy sound.

Editing is, basically, the process of editing audio files on the computer, usually using DAW programs.

Destructive Editing modifies the data of the original audio file, as opposed to just editing its playback parameters. For example, if some part of a track was deleted, it's immediately removed from that part of the track.

In *non-destructive editing*, original signal stays intact during editing, allowing the engineer to return to the original version at any time.

EDM ("Electronic dance music," "Dance music," "Club music," or just "Dance") is a broad range of electronic music genres, made mostly for festivals, nightclubs, and parties.

Effects Loop is the process of sending a signal outside your modular system, processing it through an external effects device, and bringing it back into your modular for more processing.

Effects Processor (or "Guitar Processor") is a device that adds certain audio effects (delay, overdrive, reverb, etc.) to a direct guitar signal.

Electro House is a form of house music that originated in the early 2000s. Characterized by a prominent bassline and kick drum, frequent use of samples in tracks, and tempo between 125 and 135 beats per minute (128 in most cases).

Electromagnetic Interference (or just "EMI") is a type of interference, caused by electromagnetic activity, which can be emitted by audio cables and equipment, causing unwanted noise or hum in audio systems. Common causes of EMI, in audio systems, may include computers, high-current power lines, fluorescent lighting, dimmer switches, video monitors, and radio transmitters.

Electronic Music is the music that uses electronic musical instruments and electronic music technology in its production.

Electropop is a modification of synth-pop that places more emphasis on a harder, electronic sound. This genre has seen a revival of popularity and influence since the 2000s.

Enhancer is a device that designed to brighten audio material, using some techniques, such as dynamic EQ, phase-shifting, and harmonic generation.

EP (Extended Play) is a collection of music that contains more than just a single track, but less than a full-length album (usually about 25 minutes or 4 tracks). **LP** (Long Play) is a collection of music that qualifies as a full album release (typically 40 minutes or 10 tracks at least).

Equalizer is an audio signal processor, which uses one or more filters to boost or cut the amplitude (volume) of particular frequencies within the sound. The main EQ principle is to balance or "equalize" the frequency response of an audio system or to create a balance between multiple signals in a sonic space. Equalizer helps your audio sounds better and corrects problems while recording, and also can be used to create new tonalities.

Equalization is the process of regulating the balance between frequency components within an electronic signal.

Complementary Equalization refers to equalizing sounds that share similar frequency ranges so that they complement, rather than interfere with each other. When you have indistinct sound between two instruments, you can use complementary EQ to increase a certain frequency on one instrument and lower that same frequency on the second instrument.

Equalizer types:

Active Equalizer is an equalizer that employs active components such as transistors or ICs in its processing circuits. Active EQ either boost the whole signal before the energy is released in a passive circuit, which is a part of the overall device, or boost certain frequencies through amplification rather than reducing other frequencies.

Graphic Equalizer is a type of equalizer that can regulate various frequencies of the incoming signal, using sliders that are set to specific frequency bands.

Parametric Equalizer is EQ, in which all parameters of equalization can be set to any amount, including the center frequency, the amount of cut or boost, and the bandwidth.

Passive Equalizer is a variable equalizer, requiring no power supply to operate. Consisting only of passive components (capacitors, inductors, and resistors) passive equalizers have no AC line cord. The device can only remove or subtract energy.

Semiparametric Equalizer is similar to the parametric EQ and allows you to select the frequency you want to equalize and the gain, but differs from parametric EQ in that you can't change the allocated bandwidth.

Shelving Equalizer is the basic type of EQ, which includes bass knobs and treble knobs for regulating tone control. It gives you an adjustment for highs and lows and is found in nearly all sound mixers and amplifiers. This type of equalizer is not often used in professional audio but can be an easy way to control EQ.

Sweep Equalizer is an equalizer that allows you to "sweep" or continuously vary the frequency of one or more sections.

Erosion Effect is an effect, which adds noise artifacts (sine or noise) to a particular frequency. It is very useful for enhancing sounds and getting deep, dry kicks.

Exciter ("Harmonic Exciter" or "Aural Exciter") is an audio signal processing technique, used to enhance a signal by dynamic equalization, phase manipulation, harmonic synthesis of high-frequency signals, and through the addition of subtle harmonic distortion. Also, "exciter" means a circuit that designed to enhance the presence of an audio signal, to make it sound more punchy, clear, bright, or loud.

Expander is a plug-in or signal processor that carrying the inverse function of a compressor and extending the dynamic range of an audio signal, instead of compressing it. It is achieved by further reducing the amplitude of signals that drop below the set threshold.

Fade is a gradual reduction of audio signal level, or a gradual level changing from one pre-set level to another.

Fader is a control that regulates the level (gain or attenuation) of an incoming signal to a channel on a console.

Far Field is the area away from a loudspeaker, at which the sound drops 6dB for each distance doubling, up to the critical distance. The beginning of the far field varies depending on the size of the speaker, but mostly, the far field begins from nearby 3 feet from the sound source.

Fast Mix is a particular type of DJ mix, in which a large number of tracks are merged into a single continuous mix, with only a small section from each appearing in the final work.

Feedback is the return of the output signal back, into the input of a system. It can be done in a controlled manner, through a feedback circuit to alter the sound of an instrument (most commonly analog synths or electric guitars).

Fidelity is a term, describing how accurately a sound is reproduced from its original source.

Filter is a device that removes or attenuates signals with frequencies above or below the specified cutoff frequency.

All-pass Filter means a signal processing filter that transmits all frequencies evenly in gain, but changes the phase relationship between different frequencies, changing its phase shift as a function of frequency.

Band-pass Filter is a device, plug-in or circuit that allows a narrow band of frequencies to pass through the circuit, attenuating or rejecting frequencies that are either above or below the specified range.

Band-stop Filter is a device, plug-in or circuit that attenuates a narrow band of frequencies in the signal, allowing frequencies beyond the band to pass.

Brickwall Filter is a type of low-pass filter, exhibiting a steep cutoff slope, which resembles a "brick wall."

Corner Frequency (of a filter) means the point, at which filtering begins.

High-cut Filter is a filter with a characteristic that allows all frequencies below a specified roll-off frequency to pass and attenuate all frequencies above. It can be useful on distorted sounds that are too edgy and need some smoothing out, or any other overly bright or harsh sounds.

High-pass Filter is an audio filter that attenuates signals below a particular frequency (the cut-off frequency) and transfers signals with frequencies that are higher.

Low-pass Filter is an audio filter or device that passes signals with frequencies that are lower than the cutoff and attenuates signals above the cutoff frequency.

Notch Filter is a band-stop filter, set to reject frequencies within a very narrow band. For example, a notch filter in a musical instrument amplifier may reduce frequencies in the range of 59 to 61 Hz, which is sufficient to eliminate any hum coming from the 60 Hz power line.

Reconstruction Filter is a low-pass filter on the output of a digital-to-analog converter that smoothes changes in voltage, produced by the converter, in order to eliminate clock noise from the output.

Shelving Filter removes or attenuates frequencies below or higher certain level (called "shelf").

Slot Filter is a compliment to the "notch" filter. It is a variable narrow band pass filter; capable of greater selectivity than a typical band-pass filter, by allowing only a very narrow "slot" of frequencies pass through the system.

Telephone Filter is a filter, used to simulate the sound that is heard through the phone receiver, by removing signals at frequencies lower 300 Hz and beyond 3500 Hz.

Voltage-Controlled Filter (VCF) is a filter, whose characteristics (especially the cutoff frequency) can be controlled by using a control voltage, applied to the control inputs.

Fingering, in music, is the method of using fingers in playing on an instrument and performing a piece of music.

Flanger is a modulation effect, which mixes a delayed signal with the original one. This alteration of sound causes some frequencies to be out of phase. This phase issue often called "combing," and can be very desirable if applied correctly. Flangers work almost like the phase shifters, but additionally change the pitch of the delayed signal slightly.

Flanging is an audio effect that mixes a signal with a copy of this signal, with a small-time delay. Initially, it was performed with analog recording on a magnetic tape, reproducing the original tape and a copy on two tape recorders simultaneously, and then physically pressing on the flange of one of the machines, to change the timing of the duplicate track. Nowadays, most flanging is done through digital plug-ins.

Flanking means a transmission of sound around, over, under, or through the partition or barrier, separating two spaces. Flanking sound transmission can be especially bothersome in multi-family residential buildings. The best time to guard against flanking transmission is in the design and construction phase of the dwelling.

Fletcher-Munson Curves (or "Equal Loudness Contours") is a set of graphic curves, constructed to illustrate how the human ears react to different frequencies at different loudness levels. In the 1930's Harvey Fletcher and Wilden Munson (two scientists) came to a conclusion that the way people hear specific frequencies is much more complicated than anyone previously thought. And they developed the Fletcher Munson Curve, which helps us to see how exactly frequencies are perceived. People do not hear the entire frequency range at the same loudness level. In other words, some areas of the frequency spectrum (lows, mids, or highs) may seem louder to us, than the others, and when amplitude (volume) decreases or increases, our ears hear these frequencies at different loudness levels.

FOH (Front-of-House) means the location in a venue opposite the stage, where live audio for the show is controlled and mixed.

Formants are the elements in the sound of instruments or voice that does not change frequency, as different pitches are sounded. Formants are, basically, "fixed" frequencies (or resonances) that occur as a result of the physical structure of the audio source.

Free Field, in acoustics, is a situation in which no sound reflections occur.

Frequency is a number of full cycles that sound wave (compressions and rarefactions of a medium) makes in a second (measured in Hz).

In sound, frequency defines what we hear as pitch; the longer the wavelength, the lower the cycles per second, and the smaller the pitch.

Air is a term that refers to frequencies above 12 kHz.

Center Frequency means the frequency of an audio signal that is most affected by equalizer, either attenuating or boosting the frequency.

Cutoff Frequency is a lower or upper limiting frequency.

ELF: Extremely Low Frequency (3 to 30 Hz).

Frequency Band is a continuous group (or range) of frequencies with an upper limit and a lower limit.

In analog terms, bandwidth and channel width are defined as a *frequency range*.

Frequency Doubling, caused by overloading a low-frequency speaker, makes bass instruments sound an octave higher than they really are. This is because the overloaded speaker makes the second harmonic louder than the fundamental pitch.

Frequency Modulation (FM) is a change in the frequency (pitch) of a signal. At low modulation rates, FM is perceived as vibrato or some trill, depending on the shape of the modulating waveform. When the modulating wave (MW) is in the audio range (above 20 Hz or so), FM is perceived as a change in tone color.

Frequency Response is a term described as the measure of the range of frequencies that the system is capable of producing. For example, at 20 Hz a particular input signal level may produce 100 dB of output, at 1 kHz the same input level may produce 105 dB of output, and so on.

Frequency-Shift-Key (FSK) is a protocol, in which a sync tone is recorded on a spare track of a multi-track recorder so that electronic devices (mainly drum machines) can be synchronized with the tape.

Fundamental Frequency (also called "Fundamental" or "The first harmonic of the instrument") is the lowest frequency, produced by any particular musical instrument.

Harsh is a term that described the frequencies in the 5-kHz to an 8-kHz range, which are too pronounced.

Highs ("High-End" or "High Frequencies") refer to frequencies above 4000 Hz.

Hum is a low-frequency tone that is normally a multiple of 50-60 Hz.

Lows ("Low Frequencies" or "Low-End") are the bass frequency signals, below 250 Hz.

Mids refer to the middle part of the frequency range (250 Hz - 4000 Hz).

Nyquist Frequency is a term that described as the highest frequency that can be accurately reproduced when signals are digitally encoded at a given sample rate. The Nyquist frequency, theoretically, is half of the sampling rate. If a digital recording uses a sampling rate of 44.1 kHz, for example, the Nyquist frequency will be 22.050 kHz. If the sampled signal contains frequency components that exceed the Nyquist limit, then in the digital representation of the signal will include aliasing, unless those frequencies are filtered out prior to digital encoding.

Presence Frequencies is the range of audio frequencies within 4 kHz and 6 kHz, which, when raised, can increase the sense of presence, especially on voices.

Resonant Frequency means the frequency, at which resonance occurs. The resonant frequency determines the pitch of things like recorders and other musical instruments that rely on resonant columns of air.

Roll-off Frequency is the frequency, below or above which a filter begins to filter out the harmonics of the waveform.

When the roll-off frequency rises or falls, more harmonics of sound will be filtered out.

Super High Frequency (SHF) refers to frequencies in the range between 3 GHz to 30 GHz.

Ultra High Frequency (UHF) refers to frequencies in the range between 300 MHz and 3 GHz.

Ultra Low Frequency (ULF) refers to frequencies in the range between 300 hertz and 3 kilohertz.

Upper Midrange refers to frequencies between 2 kHz and 6 kHz.

Funky House (or "Disco House") is a subgenre of house music that uses a funk or disco-inspired bass line and samples with drum breaks that draw inspiration from the 1970s and 1980s disco records.

Future Bass is a music genre that arose around 2006 in the United Kingdom, United States, China, Japan, and Australia. It is a broad genre of music with a focus on a hard bassline, offering a wide variety of rhythms and sounds, usually produced by a synthesizer on digital audio.

Future House is an electronic dance music genre that emerged in 2013, described as a fusion of deep house and modern EDM. Songs in this genre characterized by a muted melody with a frequency modulated basslines. The future house is another example of successful reworking of old ideas of the dance mainstream of the 1990s and early 2000s for their re-sale to the younger generation in our time.

FX (abbreviation for "effects") refers to the effects of every sound channel.

FX Channels are the channels that hold the effects plugin and control the return levels to the mix.

Gain is a control that can be used to boost or cut volume levels.

Gain Reduction is the action of a compressor or limiter in regulating the amplitude of an audio signal.

Garage Music is a genre of electronic dance music, originated in the early 1980s in New York, and gained popularity in the performance of musicians from New Jersey. In fact, the garage is the same classic house, but with a greater emphasis on soul and gospel vocals with saturated piano parts.

Gate (or "Noise Gate") is a plug-in or hardware device that can be configured to automatically turn off the signal during parts of the audio track, where the instruments are not played, and to activate the sound again when they start to play. Some noise gates can only be partially closed, thereby reducing the signal level, rather than suppressing it at all.

Generation is a term, used to describe the number of times that recorded audio signal has been copied.

Generation Loss is the amount of clarity lost when recorded audio is copied, due to added noise and distortion.

Gig is slang for live musical performance.

Glide (or "Portamento") is a function, in which the pitch slides smoothly from one note to the other, instead of jumping over the intervening pitches.

Glitch is a genre of electronic music that emerged in the late 1990s in Germany. Music in the style of glitch is dominated by acoustic effects, caused by errors and malfunctions in digital records - bugs (software errors), system failures, hardware noise, skip and rewind CD, and digital distortion. Instead of the bit component in the music of the glitch, there are short clicks and noises.

Goniometer is a device that used to measure angles. In audio, a goniometer is a display, which shows the correlation between the phase of two or more signals. The signals are displayed as a two-dimensional graph on two axes, which demonstrates the relationship between them. The "shape" of the display shows phase coherency. A vertical line showed 100% in-phase signals. Using a goniometer, you can determine the relative levels, stereo/surround relationship, and mono compatibility of signals.

Groove is a very mystical term. Someone says that groove is the sense of propulsive rhythmic feeling of "swing"; others say that groove is the overall impression, created by different rhythms that are being played between or within instruments; also, some people claims that groove means the whole feeling of the music. All these terms are right and correctly describe such definition as the groove, but more specifically, "groove" is the degree to which a rhythm deviates from the straight metronomic grid.

Haas Effect (also called "Precedence Effect") is a factor of human hearing, in which we perceive any sound source by its timing, rather than its sound level. Helmut Haas, in his research, determined that the first sound waves that reach our ears help our brains define where the sound is coming from, rather than its reflection or reproduction from another source. Sound reflection must be at least 10dB louder than the source or delayed by more than 30ms before it changes our perception of the direction of the sound. It helps us recognize the original sound source without being confused by reflections off of nearby surfaces.

Half Step (or "Semitone") is the smallest interval in music. In other words, it is the shortest distance between two keys on piano. It can be from black to white or white to black key.

Hamster Switch is a switch, used to reverse the channels on a crossfader. It is usually used by scratch DJ's, who find it easier to perform some tricks and scratch techniques with the crossfader this way.

Hardcore is a subgenre of EDM that distinguished from other genres by faster tempos (160 to 200 BPM or even more), the intensity of the kicks and the synthesized bass, the rhythm and the atmosphere, and the usage of saturation.

Hardstyle is an electronic dance music genre that mixing influences from hard techno and hardcore. Tracks in this genre, typically, consists of intense basslines, accompanying the beat, a deep, hard-sounding kick drum, a dissonant synth melody, and detuned and distorted sounds. The tempo in hardstyle varies between 140 to 150 beats per minute.

Harmonics: When a musical instrument is playing a note, what we are truly hearing is the fundamental pitch, which is the pitch that being played by the musical instrument, accompanied by a series of frequencies that are normally heard as a single composite tone. Those frequencies, which are integer multiples of the fundamental pitch's frequency, are called harmonics.

Even and Odd Harmonics: So, harmonic of a wave is a component frequency of the signal, which is the integer multiple of the fundamental frequency. If the fundamental frequency is f, the harmonics have frequencies f, 2f, 3f, 4f, etc., Even harmonics are 2f, 4f, 6f, and Odd harmonics are f, 3f, 5f.

Harmonic Series (or "Overtone series"): When we hear the sound from a musical instrument, we hear a sophisticated sound that contains many different frequencies or pitches. This collection of frequencies, tones or partials is called the harmonic series.

Sub Harmonics are harmonics with frequencies below the fundamental frequency. Usually, sub harmonics are multiples of 1/2, 1/3, or 1/4 of the fundamental.

Harmony is when you have several sounds, instruments, or sound sources, which are simultaneously played back to create chords and chord progressions, which have a beautiful and harmonic sound.

Headroom means a difference between normal operating level and clipping level in an amplifier or audio device (in dB).

Also, it may describe the difference between the peak levels of a recording and the point at which the signal distorts.

Head Voice (also known as "Head register") means singing in the higher part of the range.

Hearing Threshold defined as the lowest threshold of acoustic pressure sensation, possible to perceive by an organism. The hearing threshold sets the lowest limit of the hearing range.

Hemiola is a musical term for a rhythmic pattern of syncopated beats with three beats in the time of two, or two beats in the time of three.

Heterodyne: When two frequencies mix with each other through a non-linear system, difference and sum signals are produced. These signals are called "heterodynes."

Heterodyning is a signal processing technique that creates new frequencies by combining or mixing two frequencies.

Heterophony means a simultaneous performance of the same melodic line with small individual variations, by two or more performers. Such texture can be viewed, as a kind of complex monophony, in which there is only one basic melody, but which is simultaneously realized in multiple voices, each of which plays the song differently.

Hidden Track can mean:
1) A record that is not listed on the release's list;
2) A song that located before the first track on a CD (also called "pregap track");
3) One or more songs that follow different song (usually after a longer period of silence) on the same track, but not indicated on the release's list.

High Impedance (abbreviated "Hi-Z") is an impedance or resistance of several thousand ohms.

Hi-hat, in drum sets, is a double cymbal on a stand, usually positioned next to the snare.

Homophony is a musical texture of some parts, in which one melody predominates, and the other parts might be either simple chords or more intricate accompaniment pattern.

Hook is a part of a song that is easy to recognize and remember. The term "hook" goes back to the earliest days of songwriting because it relates to the part of the song, which intended to "hook" the listener: an excellent combination of lyrics, melody, and rhythm that remains in the listener's head.

House Music is electronic music genre, created by music producers and club DJs in Chicago in the early 1980s.

House music characterized by repeatable rhythm beat, usually 4/4, and sound inserts, which are repeated from time to time in music, partially coinciding with its rhythm. The tempo is generally about 118-132 BPM.

House Sync is a reference signal that is used to keep all devices in the room in sync.

Humanization is the process of making minor adjustments to the time and loudness of individual notes in a digitally quantized pattern to make it sound less robotic and add imperfections so it appears as if it was played by a human.

Hz (or "Hertz") is the unit of measurement for frequency or the number of full wave cycles that occur in a second. 1 Hz = 1 complete wave per second.

Impedance is the amount of resistance inherent in the electrical system (measured in ohms). Differences in impedance among devices in the studio can affect how they work together. The higher the impedance rating, the higher resistance is being applied to the signal, thereby causing a weaker signal to be transmitted.

Impulse Response (IR) is the response of a system to a unit impulse at its input. Whenever a system or a signal processor is given an input signal, it changes or processes the input to provide the desired output signal (depending on the system transfer function). The output of the system to a unit input signal is the impulse response of the system. The impulse response of the system assists in determining the key features and response of the system to any type of input signal.

Industrial Music refers to a genre of experimental electronic music that draws on provocative sounds and themes; originated on the middle 1970s in the United Kingdom and Germany. In general, the style is hard and challenging and defined as the most aggressive fusion of rock and electronic music.

Inharmonicity is a term described as a degree to which the frequencies of overtones depart from entire multiples of the fundamental frequency (harmonic series).

In-line Console is a mixing console, designed in such way that each channel strip can be used for both recording and monitoring purposes, during multitrack recording.

Input Gain is the volume at which a signal goes through a modifier such as an equalizer, compressor, etc.

Insert is an access in the signal chain (in the mixing console or a DAW), in which a device or digital plug-in can be "inserted" into the circuit, between pre-amplification and the channel or bus output; usually, used to add processing, such as EQ, reverb, compression to a channel or group of channels.

Instrument Out Direct is the output of an electric instrument (for example, electric guitar) directly to the recording console or tape recorder, rather than to microphone amplifier.

Intelligent Dance Music (abbreviated as "IDM") is a broad genre of electronic music that developed in the early 1990s. The term "IDM" was first invented to describe music, which was too complicated to dance to, but nowadays this term is not particularly relevant, because of the variety of music genres.

Interval is a distance between two sounds of a certain height (measured in semitones).

Intonation, in music, is a musician's realization of pitch accuracy, or the pitch accuracy of a musical instrument.

Intro is the opening section of the music track.

Inverse Square Law, as applied to sound, means that for each time you double the distance between your sound source and microphone, the power of the audio will be drop on 75%. That is why I recommend you spend some time adjusting the distance of a microphone to the source sound. A 1-feet difference can lower your signal by half.

I/O (abbreviation for "Input/Output") refers to any device, program or system involving the transferring of electrical and audio signals.

Isolation is the process of containing sound within a particular area so that it does not interact with other sounds. Acoustically treated isolation booths, for example, are often used to record vocals or instruments in the studio to keep outside noises into the recording mic or to keep vocals or other sounds away from instrument microphones, during live recording sessions.

Isomorphic Keyboard is a musical input device that consists of a two-dimensional grid of note-controlling elements (such as keys or buttons), on which any given sequence or a combination of musical intervals has the same form on the keyboard, wherever it occurs – within a key, across keys, across octaves, and across tunings.

ITB (In the Box) means producing music, engineering audio, mixing, and summing digitally within a computer. No analog hardware is used, other than an interface. It is the opposite of OTB.

Jam Session is an informal musical event, where musicians play improvised solos, melodies, and chords. To "jam" means "to improvise" music (in DAW or live) without any preparation.

Jitter means random and undesired phase or frequency deviations of the transmitted signal; time distortions of recording/playback of a digital audio signal.

Juggle is a technique, commonly used by DJs, to rearrange musical samples in that way so that it sounds like something new.

Jungle (or "Oldschool Jungle") is a genre of electronic music, derived from old school hardcore, which developed in England in the early 1990s. This style characterized by rapid tempos (150 to 200 bpm) and breakbeats, heavily syncopated percussive loops, samples, and synthesized effects.

Key can mean:
1) The note scale, in which a part of music (written or played) identified by the first note (tonic) of the scale;
2) A button or lever that transfers a signal or performs an action, such as the keys on a keyboard;
3) A control of a dynamic processing device by an external audio signal ("key input").

Keyboard Controller is a piano-styled keyboard that sends out MIDI signals to control other MIDI devices.

Keytar is a lightweight electronic keyboard that is supported by a strap around the neck and shoulders (similar to a guitar). Keytar gives players a greater range of movement onstage, compared to conventional keyboards.

kHz is an abbreviation for "kilohertz" (1000 Hz, or 1000 cycles per second; for example, 3000 Hz = 3 kHz). It is usually used in the studio, for describing audio frequency ranges or digital sampling rates.

Kill Switch is a switch or button to turn on/off output or individual frequency ranges within a channel (lows, mids, and highs).

Knee is the point, at which a response or function makes a change. The term is used in particular with a compressor, where the threshold setting determines the point, at which compression begins.

Hard Knee refers to a more abrupt introduction of compression of the signal, once the sound level crosses the threshold.

Soft Knee refers to the gradual introduction of compression of the signal, once the sound level crosses the threshold.

Latency: How long it takes for sound to reach your ears from a particular audio source. For example, if the latency of your MIDI keyboard is low, then after pressing a key you will immediately hear a sound, without any delays.

Layering refers to almost any blending of similar multiple audio parts or sounds at once, often combined on one channel. In the audio recording, layering usually involves recording similar parts of the same instrument (or duplicating parts with small delays or chorusing effects) to create richer and brighter sound.

Level is the amount of signal strength.

LFE (Low-Frequency Effects) **Channel** is the name of an audio track, specifically intended for low-pitched and deep sounds ranging from 3-120 Hz. This track is normally sent to a speaker that is specially designed for low-pitched sounds called the subwoofer.

Limiter is a type of compressor that sharply decreases (limits) the gain of the signal when the audio level achieves a particular threshold, usually used to prevent overload and signal peaking. A compressor completely becomes a limiter when its ratio is 10:1 or higher.

Line Level is the standard audio signal level that goes through interconnecting cables in the recording studio or sound system before a signal is expanded and sent to the speakers.

Loop is a section of some music part, cut in such a way, that it can be endlessly repeated. Loops can vary from a few seconds to many minutes in length, and can also be used by composers for producing a quick and convenient underscore, from which many compositions can be created, often with drum and bass line loops.

Loudness is a term, referring to how the human ear perceives incoming sound waves. We commonly think of loudness as it associates to the volume of a sound, but this is an indirect relationship. In acoustics, a volume is more about the amplitude of the sound waves, and loudness defines how our ears hear the energy of those waves.

Low Fidelity ("Lo Fi," "Low-Fidelity" or "Lo-Fi") is a type of sound recording, which contains technical flaws that make the recording sound different, compared to the live sound being recorded, such as distortion, background noise, or limited frequency response.

Low-Frequency Oscillator (LFO) emits low-frequency electronic waveforms, below the audible level of human hearing (20 Hz or less). This low-frequency waveform generates a rhythmic pulse that is used to modulate various parameters of the audio signal, such as volume or pitch. LFOs are commonly employed in samplers, synthesizers and signal processors to create such effects as tremolo, vibrato, phasing, etc.

Low Impedance (or "Lo-Z") is the impedance of 500 ohms or less.

Major and Minor is a musical composition, movement, section, scale, chord, key, or interval. If we talk about keys, the easiest way to recognize the difference between major and minor is to consider the emotion their music evoke– **Minor keys** have a melancholy and morose sound, while **Major keys** are all about bright and happy melody.

Mapper is a device that translates MIDI data from one form to another, in real time.

Mash-up is very similar to a DJ mix but differs from it in that two or more songs are playing simultaneously, and not one after the other. In a mash-up, each source will contribute more-or-less equally to the final work. A standard mash-up technique is to use music from one song mixed with the vocals of another.

Masking is a characteristic of hearing, by which loud sounds prevent the ear from hearing softer sounds with the same frequency. It also refers to the obscuring of softer sounds by louder ones.

Master is the final-mixed original recording, from which other copies are made.

Master Channel is where your signal goes before it leaves your system, and where you mix all your tracks in a project.

Master Fader can mean:
1) The fader, which controls the primary output of the console during mixdown;
2) Faders, in some consoles, which control the outputs to the multitrack tape recorder during recording;

3) Sometimes used to mean a VCA master (one slide that controls the control voltage, sent to several VCA faders).

Mastering is the final process of fine-tuning and "sweetening" your tracks, before its distribution. Mastering adds the final audio touch to an already mixed song, which is a stereo track. The primary mastering goal is matching a song's acoustic character to that of other songs on the same album, optimizing volume, and adding the last 5% of sonic enhancement (treble, bass, clarity, wideness). Mastering takes less time than mixing and makes less of a difference in the general sound of your song, but is still vital, as a finishing touch.

Mastertrack controls the overall playback volume, changes size and tempo of the whole track, and dedicated to creating your final stereo mix.

Medley is a musical composition, consisting of several different songs that have been rearranged into one continuous track.

Metadata is the information about the track, such as track name, descriptions, keywords, writers, genres, and BPM.

Metronome is a device that generates audible beats, clicks, or another sound at regular intervals that users can set in BPM.

Microphone is a transducer that transforms sound pressure waves into electrical signals.

> *Diaphragm* is the part of a microphone that moves in response to sound waves, converting them into electrical signals.

> *Gobo* is a portable isolation panel, used to reduce sound leakage between microphones.

On Axis is the position right in front of the microphone diaphragm, in line with its movement.

Shock Mounts are used for reducing the acoustic coupling of the microphone stand to the microphone. Mechanical vibrations on a stage or other unwanted sounds are often transmitted to the microphone from the stand, and shock mounts have excellently reduced these adverse effects.

Main microphone types:

Cardioid Microphone captures all sounds ahead and blocks everything else. This allows you to point the mic at the sound source and isolates it from unwanted surrounding sounds, what makes it perfect for live performances.

Condenser Microphone is a microphone, in which sound is transformed into electrical current through some changes in a capacitor. The sound pressure waves move the diaphragm, generating changes in capacitance, which are then changed into electrical voltage.

Contact Microphone is a microphone that picks up vibrations from solid objects (as opposed to vibrations in the air). Unlike traditional air microphones, contact microphones are insensitive to air vibrations and transduce only structure-borne sound.

Dynamic Microphone is a microphone, in which sound pressure waves converted to an electrical sound signal, by an induction coil, moving in a magnetic field. Dynamic microphones are less sensitive than condenser mics, but can be useful with louder sound sources.

Omnidirectional Microphone captures sound from all sides. Due to its non-directivity and zero rejection, this microphone better reflects nuances, which leads to a more natural sound.

Ribbon Microphone is a microphone that converts sound waves to electrical current through a thin conductive ribbon, set between magnetic poles.

Supercardioid Microphone has the same front directionality as cardioid, but has a narrower area of sensitivity. It results in improved insulation and higher resistance to feedback. Because of their increased ability to reject noise, you can use them for loud sound sources, noisy scenes or even for unprocessed recording rooms.

Zoom Microphone is a type of mic with three cardioid microphone components and a particular phase correction equalization circuit. By adjusting the control knob, the mic output can be varied from omnidirectional through cardioid to supercardioid.

Microtones (or "Microintervals") are the intervals that smaller than a semitone.

Middle-8 is a part of a song that lasts eight beats.

MIDI (Musical Instrument Digital Interface) is a digital data protocol, which allows electronic music instruments to connect and communicate with one another.

All-notes-off is a MIDI command that causes any notes that are currently sounding to be shut off.

MIDI Controller can mean:
1) A device or software that transmits MIDI data to connected devices, both through pre-programmed sequencing or through live performance by a musician;
2) Any of controls on a MIDI device that is assigned to control specific parameters of the sound.

MIDI Interface is a device that transforms a MIDI signal into the digital format of a computer, so that it can store and use this MIDI signal.

MIDI Sample Dump Standard (SDS) is a sub-protocol that was added into MIDI to allow the transfer of digitally recorded samples among the instruments, storage units or sound modules, without turning them to analog.

MIDI Sequencer is a device or software that can record and play back MIDI data.

MIDI Time Code (MTC) means a translation of the information in SMPTE time code into MIDI data, allowing MIDI sequencers and connected devices to synchronize with SMTPE code.

Mix is the blending of audio signals together into one composite signal.

Mixdown (or "Mix Down") is the processes of producing a final mix by combining multiple audio tracks into a single track, before the mastering stage.

Mixer is a console (or a section of a console) that blends multiple audio signals into a composite signal.

Mixing is a vital step in music production. Mixing happens after all the elements are already recorded, and involves: balancing levels of all of the separately recorded tracks, placing each instrument in the stereo spectrum, processing and enhancing each track's audio character, and adding creative effects to make your song more interesting, cohesive, and polished. Mixing has a huge effect on the final sound of your song.

Mixing Console is an electronic device for blending, routing, and changing the volume level, timbre, and dynamics of many different audio signals.

Mixing Engineer is a person responsible for mixing the various sound elements of a piece of recorded music (instruments, vocals, effects, etc.) into a final version of a song.

Modulation refers to any process, in which a value of one signal is affected by the adding another signal. In audio, this leads to a change in sound. **Modulation effect** delays an audio signal and shifts (modulate) it when the delayed signal plays back relative to the original signal.

Monaural means an audio signal, coming through a single channel. Also, monaural sound is a single channel or track of sound created by one speaker and is also known as "Monophonic sound" or "High-fidelity sound."

Monitor Mix is a mix, created to allow musicians to hear themselves, whether onstage or in the studio. Monitor mixes are on an individual signal path from the main mix and do not affect the signal, going into the DAW.

Monitor Path is a signal path, separate from the channel path, which allows sound engineer to listen to what is being recorded, without "touching" and changing the signal being fed to the multitrack recorder or DAW.

Monitors are the speakers (or headphones) in the studio that is used to listen to audio signals, mainly for the purpose of checking sound quality.

Monody is a musical style, employing a single melodic line without accompaniment.

Monophonic (or "Mono") can mean:
1) A line of melody, in which only one note is played;
2) A single sound source or single-channel transmission (as opposed to stereo);
3) An instrument or synthesizer setting that plays only one pitch at a time.

Monophony is the simplest of musical texture, consisting of a melody, typically played by a single instrument player, or sung by a solo singer, without accompanying harmony or chords.

Morphing is a sound effect that imposes the characteristics of one sound on

another. In music production, morphing is usually used to solve two types of tasks:
1) Getting a smooth shift between the two sounds;
2) Creating a new sound that has the characteristics of the original two sounds.

MP3 (MPEG-1 Audio Layer 3) is a digital audio format and technology that is used for compressing a sound to a smaller file but still preserving the original audio quality.

MPEG2 is an audio format; compared to MP3, MPEG2 provides better quality music, compressed to 70% of its original size, and held up to 48 audio channels, and sample rates up to 96 kHz.

Multitimbral is the ability of a synthesizers, samplers, or music workstations to play several various sounds, patches or timbres at once.

Multitrack Recording (also called "tracking" or "multitracking") means the process of recording a group of sound sources onto separate tracks and then combining them to play back simultaneously.

Near Field is the area between 1-5 feet from the source of a sound. Studio monitors are, ordinarily, considered "near-field" speakers, because they are intended to be listened to at the close distance.

Needle can mean:
1) The part of a record deck that touches the vinyl and transforms a changing surface of the record into vibration;
2) A term, referring to a turntable's stylus.

Negative Feedback is a part of the output signal that is fed back to an input of the amplifier with its phase inverted from the initial output signal.

Node (in sound) is a point, line or surface in a standing wave where the wave has minimum amplitude. **Antinode** is a point, line or surface in a standing wave where the wave has maximum amplitude.

Noise describes any unwanted or unintended sound frequencies, present in the audio signal.

Ambient Noise Level is the level of acoustic noise existing in a given area.

Noise Floor is the level of noise, present in the audio signal (measured in dB). Every electronic device emits a minimum degree of noise, even when no sound is passing through it; the lower the noise floor in these devices, the higher the quality of the device.

Noise Gating is the process of sound suppression, typically, after the signal falls below a specified level. Noise gating is helpful to mute low-level hums, frequently found in recordings made at live gigs.

Noise Rating (NR) is a system for evaluating the noise in space, which determines the acceptable indoor environment for hearing preservation.

Noise Reduction means removing noise from a signal, device or system.

Noise Reduction Coefficient (NRC) is a specification for the effectiveness of acoustic absorption materials, obtained by averaging the absorption coefficients across the range of frequency bands.

Noise Shaping is an audio tool for producing digital dither, allowing added noise to be changed into those components of the audio spectrum, where the human ears are less sensitive.

Colors of noise:

Black Noise is, basically, a silence. It has a frequency spectrum of predominantly zero power level over all frequencies except for a few narrow bands or spikes.

Blue Noise (or "Azure Noise") is a type of noise, whose power density (spectral loudness) increases 3 dB per octave with increasing frequency. Because blue noise is biased toward higher frequencies, it sounds like a high-pitched hiss with a lack of bass. Blue noise gets its name from optics, as the color blue is on the higher end of the frequency spectrum for visible light.

Brownian Noise (or "Brown Noise") is a type of noise that has a spectral density that's inversely proportional to its frequency squared. In other words, its power decreases significantly with increasing frequency, and as a result, brown noise has much more energy at lower frequencies than at higher frequencies.

Grey Noise is random noise, whose frequency spectrum is perceived by the listener as equally loud at all frequencies. The result is that grey noise contains all frequencies with equal loudness, as opposed to white noise, which contains all frequencies with equal energy, but is not perceived as being equally loud due to biases in the human equal-loudness contour.

Pink Noise ("Flicker Noise" or "1/f noise") is a noise signal, similar to white noise, which contains all audible frequencies but with equal energy per octave, unlike all frequency bands. Engineers often use pink noise as a tool for tuning and calibrating sound equipment. The frequency spectrum of pink noise is linear in logarithmic scale; it has equal power in bands that are proportionally wide. This means that pink noise would have equal power in the frequency range from 40 to 60 Hz as in the band from 4000 to 6000 Hz. The spectral power density, compared with white noise, decreases by 3 dB per octave (density proportional to 1/f). That's why pink noise is often called "1/f noise."

Red Noise is random noise, in which the energy content is reduced by 6 dB per octave, thus having most of its energy in the low frequencies; similar to pink noise, but with different spectral content and different relationships (i.e. 1/f for pink noise, $1/f^2$ for red noise).

Violet Noise (or "Purple noise") is a type of noise, which power density increases 6 dB per octave with increasing frequency. It is also known as differentiated white noise, due to its being the result of the differentiation of a white noise signal.

White Noise is a noise signal (generally from 20Hz to 20kHz) that contains an equal spread of energy overall audible frequencies. From an energy point of view, white noise has a constant power per hertz (also called a unit bandwidth), i.e., at each frequency there is the same amount of power.

Other types of noise:

Asperity Noise is a type of noise, caused by minute imperfections in the surface of a recording medium (tape); heard as a low-frequency rumble, similar to rocks banging together.

Background Noise is any type of noise that is not the sound that you are specifically listening to.

Broadband Noise (or "Wideband noise") is a noise, the energy of which is distributed over a wide section of the audible range as opposed to narrowband noise.

Friction Noise refers to frequency modulation of the signal in the range above about 100 Hz resulting in distortion, which can be perceived as a noise added to the signal (i.e., a noise not present in the absence of a signal).

Impulse Noise includes unwanted, almost instantaneous sharp sounds, usually caused by electromagnetic interference, scratches on the recording disks, explosions, and bad synchronization in digital recording and communication.

Inherent Noise ("Self noise" or "Residual noise") means noise level of a microphone when no signal is present.

Intermittent Noise is a noise level that increases and decreases rapidly.

Line Noise refers to any noise that occurs in the electric power supply when other equipment, normally within the same facility, is switched on or off.

Masking Noise is a noise that is intense enough to make another sound (that is also present) unintelligible or inaudible.

Modulation Noise is the noise that is present only when the audio signal is present.

Narrowband Noise is a noise that occurs over a limited frequency range.

Popcorn Noise is a type of noise, which primarily found in integrated circuit audio amplifiers that make a sizzling sound, similar to popcorn popping.

Print-through is a category of noise, caused by contact transfer of signal patterns from one layer of magnetic tape to another.

Quantization Noise is the modulation noise in a signal, resulting from quantization error.

Residual Noise means a noise level that left on recording tape after it has been erased.

Thermal Noise is a type of noise, which appearing in electronic circuits and devices as a result of the temperature-dependent random motions of electrons and other charge carriers.

Weighted Noise means a noise, measured within the audio frequency range using a selective frequency measuring device.

Noise Music is a category of music that is characterized by the expressive use of noise as a primary music aspect.

Normalization, basically, means an increasing the volume of a piece of audio to raise the maximum peak level. Normalization a set of tracks to a common level ensures that the loudest peak in each track is the same. Nowadays, normalization is one of the functions in most digital audio workstations.

Notch means a narrow band of audio frequencies.

Note, in music, is the pitch and duration of a sound, and also its representation in musical notation.

Brown Note is a mythical note with a very low frequency (5-9 Hz, that's well below human hearing).

Dyad is a set of two musical notes or pitches.

Ghost Note is a music note with rhythmic value, but no discernible pitch. Also, ghost note can be described as a random note, created while playing a MIDI instrument, when the note is not pressed hard enough to be heard.

Grace Note is an extra note that not essential to the harmony or melody, not counted in rhythm and added as an embellishment.

Leading Note is a note or pitch, which "leads" a note one semitone lower or higher, being a lower and upper leading-tone, respectively.

Root Note means a pitch, upon which a chord is based; the fundamental note, on top of which the intervals of a chord are built.

Object-based Audio (OBA) is a method of producing surround sound, in which sounds are directed to a certain point in space, rather than a particular speaker or set of speakers.

Octave is an interval or difference of pitch of 12 half-steps.

Offbeat is a beat between the main beats.

Omni is a prefix that means "all."

Omni Mode is a setting that allows a MIDI device to identify and respond to all MIDI channels at once.

OSC (an abbreviation for "Open Sound Control") is a protocol for communicating sound synthesizers, computers, and other multimedia devices.

Oscillator is a tone generator in a synthesizer. Also, oscillator means a device that puts out test tones at various frequencies.

OTB (Out the Box) means mixing and summing audio outside the computer, using analog equipment. It is the opposite of ITB.

Output Level is the signal level at the output of a device.

Outro is the end of a song or track.

Overdubbing is the process of recording an additional audio track (or tracks) over an existing recording. Overdubbing allows monitoring one or more of previously recorded tracks, while simultaneously recording several signals onto other tracks. This technique can be repeated until the song has been built up.

Overtone is any harmonic in a tone, except the fundamental frequency. Also, overtones are the set of all partials, present in the sound, excluding the fundamental.

Pad is a device or circuit that attenuates the incoming signal, generally to prevent overload of an amplifier, which follows along the path of a signal.

Paraphonic Synth is a synth, in which all of the notes being played go through a single filter (VCF) and amplifier (VCA).

Partial is any of the simple tones (or sine waves), of which a complex tone is made. You can take any complex waveform and break it down into a set of individual sine waves with various frequencies and amplitudes, each representing a particular pitch and relative loudness. Those individual sine waves are called partials. This concept is an essential part of producing sounds in synthesizers; in additive synthesis, some number of partials is combined to generate a particular tone.

Pan (or "Panning") is the process of "placing" a certain sound within the stereo field. It is achieved by controlling the balance of the signal between the right and left speakers.

Pass Band is the frequency range of signals that will be "passed" by a filter, rather than reduced.

Patch can mean:
1) Some sound setting or program on a synthesizer;
2) To route (or reroute) the signal in audio system, by using short cables with plugs inserted into jacks.

PCM (Pulse Code Modulation) is a standard method of encoding analog audio signals in a digital form.

Peak Limiter is a compressor with a quick attack time, medium and fast release time, a high ratio, and high threshold. The primary peak limiter task is to stop or monitor only the very quick, sudden peak levels that will overload the next stage of the audio signal.

Peak Meter is a meter, which determines an absolute peak value of a waveform.

Peak Response refers to the amplitude of an audio signal at its maximum value.

Peak-to-Peak (pk-pk) is the difference between the maximum positive and the maximum negative amplitudes of a waveform.

Peak Value (or "Peak Level") is the measure of the maximum negative or positive amplitude of a waveform at any moment. In audio, it is visually represented as the farthest point of the waveform below or above zero axis.

Pentatonic Scale is a term that refers to the musical scale with five notes per octave, in opposite to a heptatonic (seven-note) scale, such as the major and minor scale.

Percussion is a musical instrument (such as a drum, cymbal or timpani) sounded as a result of a striking, shaking or scraping.

Phase is a measurement of the time difference between two similar waveforms.

Phase Inversion can be described as polarity inversion. Musical waves have positive and negative parts. The positive part of wave corresponds to the increase in air compression, while the negative part compares with a reduction in air pressure (or rarefaction, which is the opposite of compression). Considering that waves are asymmetrical, the positive and negative parts are not mirrors of each other, so when polarity is reversed by some part or component in the recording chain, the positive and negative parts of the wave are shifted. The compression wave becomes a rarefaction and vice versa. In many recordings and components, polarity gets reversed, and phase inversion provides a way to correct this.

Phaser uses sets of all-pass filters that leave the sound intact, but add sweepable phase shifts. That phase shifted channels will then be mixed through VCAs with the original signal. It works like a comb filter with a slow resonance, which pulsing over the frequencies. **Phasing effect** is achieved whenever an original waveform is combined (usually 50/50) with the other, slightly time-shifted version of it. In fact, the offset in time of the duplicate version is so small in actual phasing effect, that instead of using a delay line, an all-pass filter is used. Filters enter a phase shift (hence the name of this effect) of 90° or more, depending on the slope.

In all-pass filter, the point is not so much to filter out a particular range of frequencies, but to use the proper phase shift for any creative purposes.

Phon is a unit of apparent loudness, numerically equal to the same number of dB as a tone playing at 1000 Hz.

Phrase: Just like the bits are grouped together into bars, the bars themselves are grouped into phrases.

Piano Roll, in a DAW, is the part of software where you can edit MIDI notes. The Piano roll's purpose is to send note and automation data to plugin instruments loaded on the Piano roll's Channel. Note pitch is displayed on the vertical axis and time on the horizontal axis. Note data can be entered manually with the editing tools or recorded in from home or studio MIDI controllers, then edited to fix mistakes and make some changes.

Pitch is a property of sound that allows you to classify a sound as relatively high or low. Pitch defined by the frequency of sound wave vibrations.

Pitch Bend is a mechanism on a synth, controller or keyboard that can cause the note's pitch to move up or down by a small amount.

Pitch Shifting is a sound effect, which allows you to shift the pitch and transform one sound (or voice) into entirely different one. Effects units that increase or lower pitch by a pre-designated musical interval are termed "pitch shifters" or "pitch benders."

Pitch-to-MIDI Converter (or "Audio-to-MIDI Converter") is a device that identifies pitch in an analog audio signal and translates it into MIDI information.

Pitch-to-Voltage Converter is a device that defines the frequency of an audio waveform and transforms it into a control voltage, which, in turn, is fed to an oscillator that generates a pitch at the same frequency.

Pitch Wheel is a switch on a synthesizer that raises or lowers the pitch of the notes being sounded.

Podcast is a digital audio file of information or a program that can be downloaded from internet to computer, frequently presented as a series of programs, to which people can subscribe and listen to on a regular basis.

Pole is a portion of filter circuit. The more poles that filter have, the sharper its cut-off slope will be. Each pole produces a slope of 6dB per octave; standard filter configurations are two-pole (12dB/oct) and four-pole (24dB/oct).

Polyphony is a style of a musical composition, employing two or more simultaneous but relatively independent melodic lines.

There are two types of polyphony:

Imitative - a song begins in one voice and then overlapped by a second voice, which singing the same melody;

Non-imitative - two or more different songs are performed at the same time.

Polyrhythm is a simultaneous use of two or more conflicting rhythms, which are hardly perceived as deriving from one another.

Pop Filter is a device that is disposed between the microphone and vocalist to prevent loud "pop" sounds, created by the singer's breath directed toward the microphone.

Portamento is a musical term, referring to the gliding effect that lets a sound to change pitch at a gradual speed, rather than abruptly.

Post-fader relates to an aux send position that places the send after the volume fader, so volume changes are reflected in this send, unlike to pre-fader.

Post-production, in recording, is the process that occurs after primary recording and includes such things as additional overdubs, editing, mixing, and mastering.

Potentiometer (or "Pot") is, generally, any mechanism that controls input or output voltage, by changing amounts (for example, volume control or the number of a signal sent to an aux send). Potentiometers can be faders or knobs, meaning that almost every control on a console that isn't a switch or a button - is a potentiometer.

PPQ (Pulses per Quarter-note) is a common measure of a sequencer's clock resolution.

Preamplifier (or simply "Preamp") is an electronic amplifier that transforms a weak electrical signal into an output signal, powerful enough, to be noise-tolerant, and vigorous enough for further processing or for sending to power amplifier and loudspeaker. All of the filtering elements can add some noise to your system and by adding a preamp, those noises in the filtering will be minimized. Also, the preamp can act as a simple buffer within your source and the filtering equipment. Microphone preamp also has the feature of amplifying the low input voltage into a more general level.

Pre-dubbing is the process of mixing sound elements, creating stems of dialogue, music, and sound effects, so that the final mix involves less work.

Pre-emphasis refers to a boosting of high frequencies during the recording process to keep the audible signal above the noise floor.

Pre-fade Listen (PFL) is a function on the channel strip of mixer or DAW, which enables channel signal to be heard and frequently metered, before the channel fader.

Pre-fader relates to an aux send position that places the send before the volume fader, so any volume changes, which made on the fader, are not reflected in the send (unlike to post-fader).

Pre-mastering is the process that precedes mastering and include such thing as checking the recording for errors and artifacts, and the overall compression and the equalization of the recording (you need to make sure that the song sounds "thicker," "wider," "bigger," "brighter" and, of course, louder).

Premixes are the cut sound elements, which divided in such a way, that if any part needs to be changed or deleted, it can be done without damaging other sounds.

Pre-production is the process of planning the track, drawing up an approximate idea of how it will look, writing a draft, choosing the right tempo and setting up the equipment before production.

Presence is the amplification of the upper-mid frequencies to cause a sound or instrument to cut through, which creates the impression that the sound source is "present" next to the listener.

Preset is a built-in sound (in a synthesizers or software plugins) that was programmed by the manufacturer of the device. Most synths come with a lot of presets to show the capabilities of the instrument and provide users with starting points for their works.

Progressive House is a subgenre of house music, originated in the early 1990's in the UK. Progressive House characterized by a large number of samples and musical instruments in the development of rhythm, and a richer sound, but the key features of the house - the standard size 4/4 and the tempo (120-140 BPM) still remains.

Protocol is a set of rules that regulate the structuring and transmitting of data in a standardized format, so all connected devices can correctly interpret the data.

Proximity Effect, in audio, refers to increasing in low-frequency (or bass) response, when a sound source is close to the microphone.

PSG (Programmable Sound Generator) is an audio chip that generates sound waves, by synthesizing various underlying waveforms (and also some noises), and connecting and mixing these waveforms into a single complex waveform, then forms the amplitude of the resulting waveform, using ADSR time periods, so that the resulting waveform then simulates a particular sound.

Psychedelic Trance ("psy" or "psytrance") is a subgenre of trance music, which offers variety regarding mood, tempo, and style and characterized by arrangements of synthetic rhythms and layered melodies, created by high tempo riffs.

Public Domain refers to any material not protected by copyright and therefore available for use without the approval of the copyright holders.

Pulse-Width Modulation (PWM) varies the ratio of time, spent in the "high" state of sound waveform versus the "low" state. It means that you get a moving vertical edge in the waveform, which can give the illusion of an additional detuned pitch at high rates, and phasing sound at slow rates.

Punch-in is an "old-school" recording term that refers to the process of recording a short section of audio "over" a previously recorded part.

Pure Tone is a tone, consisting of only the fundamental frequency, with no overtones or harmonics, graphically represented as a simple sine wave.

Q ("Quality Factor" or "Q Factor") define the bandwidth of frequencies that will be impacted by an equalizer. The lower the Q, the larger the bandwidth curve of frequencies that will be cut or boosted.

Quadraphonic is now a rarely-used system of four-channel sound, where the channels are indicated as right front, right back, left front, and left back, dedicated to delivering sound from all four corners of a room.

Quantization can mean:
1) The process of regulating the timing of played notes, so that they fall precisely on

a grid or bars and beats. This method is used to ensure that each note is played exactly where it should be played, and not behind or ahead of the rhythm. Most DAWs are also had a quantize setting, which allows you to pull the notes from where they were played in, and move them closer to the grid;

2) The process of transforming a continuous analog audio signal to a digital signal with discrete numerical values. For example, in CD an analog recording is converted into a digital signal, sampled at 44, 1 Hz, and quantized with 16-bits of data per sample.

Radio Edit is, normally, a version of a song, made specifically for radio (the song has probably been reduced to approximately 3 minutes).

Rarefaction is the reduced density of air particles, during the trough of a sound wave. It is the opposite of compression.

Ratcheting is a kind of trick, used with sequencers, where one stage of the sequence may be triggered quickly multiple times. It is usually used to produce a sharp, quick, percussion sound, creating an effect, sometimes referred to as the "squeaky door sound."

Ratio determines the amount of dynamic processing that happens to the signal.

Rave is any gathering of people, centered around listening to and dancing to electronic music, as played by a set of live DJs.

Recording Bus is a bus that sends mix signals from the console channels to the multitrack recorder or DAW.

Recording Session is a period, in which music is being recorded in the studio.

Reference Level is a standard baseline level of volume, used to measure how much level is present (in dB) below or above the baseline.

Reference Tone is a single-frequency tone, used to calibrate the levels of sound equipment and to set reference level.

Reflection is the bouncing of sound waves off a flat surface, as opposed to absorption. Reflected sounds from a distance are perceived as echo, while reverberation is created from thousands of reflections.

Refraction of sound is a bending of sound rays in nonuniform medium, such as the atmosphere or the ocean, in which the speed of sound depends on the coordinates. Refraction, or bending of the path of the waves, is accompanied by a change in speed and wavelength of the waves. The more rapid the change in the speed of sound, the more pronounced the refraction.

Refrain, in a song, is a phrase or line, which repeats at the end of the verse.

Release Time is the time, during which the output signal returns to the original levels when the input signal crosses the specified threshold.

Remastering can mean:
1) The process of creating new stuff from the same original raw audio material;
2) A method when an old song (or a part of a track) is taken, and with the help of modern music production and recording techniques, it becomes brighter, more saturated, and fresh.

Rendering is the process of converting one or more tracks in your project into a sound file format.

Resampling can mean:
1) A process, by which the sampling rate of a piece of audio is converted to another sampling rate;

2) A process of taking a piece of audio (with a chain of effects on it) and bouncing out the result as audio.

Reverberation (or "Reverb") simulates the sound of acoustic environments, such as rooms, concert halls, caverns, or the sound of infinite space. The familiar sound of clapping in some empty room is a good example of reverb. In any acoustic space, sounds echo off the surfaces of the space (the floor, walls, and ceiling) over and over, and then gradually fade out. **Reverberation effect** consists of thousands of delays, of different lengths and intensities, which simulate these natural echoes. Reverberation adds a sense of space and natural sounding depth to your sounds and can be used to simulate both fantastic and realistic acoustic environments.

Dereverberation means the processing of an audio signal to reduce or eliminate reverberation.

Early Reflection is the first stage of reverberation. In other words, early reflections are the first sound waves that reach your ear after bouncing off a surface.

Plate Reverb is a device that produces artificial reverberation by sending vibrations across a metal plate, through a transducer, which is similar to a speaker driver.

Reverb Chamber is a device, built to simulate room reflections.

Reverb Density refers to the density of a reverb effect. Generally, the lower the density, the grainier or more diffuse the reverb tail will sound, due to the thinness of the echoes; the higher the density, the smoother reverb tail, due to the thickness of the echoes.

Reverb Envelope is the ADSR of the reverb volume, or how quickly the reverb reaches the peak level and the rate of its attenuation.

Reverb Field is a space that is far enough from the sound source that the reverb is louder than the direct sound.

Reverb Hall is the reverb, heard in a concert hall. The construction of a music hall produces a reverb that lasts anywhere from 1 to 3 seconds or longer.

Reverb Tail is a gradually fading echo or after-sound.

Reverb Time (RT) is the time it takes for reverberations or sound echoes to disappear after the direct sound has stopped.

Spring Reverb is a device that simulates reverberation by producing vibrations within a metal spring, by adding it to a transducer and sending an audio signal through it. Nowadays, most studios emulate spring reverb with the use of plugins or hardware reverb units.

Rewind, in DJs slang, means to rewind the song to the beginning, to reproduce it again because the crowd liked it.

RF Interference is the unwanted noise, introduced into electronics, circuits, or audio systems by the presence of RF signals.

Rhythm Section is the musical instruments in a band or ensemble that are responsible for performing rhythmic parts, instead of melody parts. In modern music, rhythm sections, usually, consist of drums and bass, along with some combination of percussion, piano, and guitars.

Rhythm Tone is a guitar tone that is used for comping chord parts and rhythmic background parts.

Riff is a short melody, repeatedly played in tune, often with variation between vocal lines.

Ring Modulator is a special type of mixer that accepts two signals as audio inputs and outputs their sum and difference tones, but does not pass on the frequencies, found in the original signals themselves.

Riser (or "Buildup") is a section of the song with progressively increasing tension to create energy in preparation of the drop or "sound explosion." This term, usually, related only to electronic music.

Rise Time is the rate, at which an audio waveform sharply increases the amplitude.

Roll-off is a decrease in the signal level when the signal frequency deviates from the cut-off frequency.

Roll-off Slope is the acuity of a filter's cutoff frequency; measured in decibels (dB) per octave.

Routing is a mixer function that allows you to direct the source signals to internal buses or external processing units and effects.

RPM is an abbreviation for "Revolutions per Minute" (a number of times the record revolves in any given minute).

Rumble refers to a low-frequency sound from the bearings inside a turntable.

Sabin is a unit used to measure sound absorption. Sabines can be imperial as well as metric units. One sabin means the absorption of one square foot of 100% absorbing material.

Sample can mean:
1) A short section of audio, recorded for the purpose of reproducing and managing the sound digitally;
2) In digital recording, a sample is the numerical measure of the waveform level, at a given moment of time. Analog music is digitally represented by many samples, taken in quick succession.

Sampler is a device that records and plays samples, often with features for editing, managing and storing the samples.

Sampling, in audio, is a process of converting a signal into a numeric sequence. In other words, it means converting real sounds into a form that computer can store and replay.

A/D (Analog to Digital Conversion), in audio, refers to converting recorded sound from electrical voltages to digital data. An A/D converter works by "sampling" sound wave at regular intervals. At each sampling, it samples the wave and turns it into a number for computer (0 or 1).

D/A (an abbreviation for "Digital to Analog Conversion") changes digital data numbers (digital audio signal) into the discrete voltage level; the reverse process of A/D.

Downsampling means a decreasing digital audio signal, by lowering its sampling rate or sample size. Downsampling is done to reduce the bit rate when transmitting over a limited bandwidth, or to convert to a more limited audio format. Downsampling is the opposite of Upsampling.

Interpolation Sampling is a type of sampling, in which the melody of a source is copied, rather than use the original audio (to avoid the copyrights).

Oversampling is a term that refers to using a higher sampling rate than needed, to start the A/D either D/A converter, thus raising the rate of the signal. Also, upsampling is a rate conversion from one rate to another random rate.

Sample Rate determines the number of samples taken per second by an A/D converter. The higher a sample rate, the more realistic the digital reproduction of the sound can be, and the higher sound frequencies can be reproduced.

Sample Rate Conversion is the conversion of digital audio, taken at one sample rate to a different sampling frequency, without first transforming the signal to analog.

Undersampling ("Bandpass sampling" or "Harmonic sampling") is a technique, in which one samples a bandpass-filtered signal at a sampling frequency below its Nyquist frequency.

Upsampling is a technique of increasing the sample rate (for example from 42.1 kHz to 84.2 kHz) and adding new samples in-between existing samples, to make a higher quality digital audio signal. The sample size is also increasing for more precise detail. The objective is to get a smoother digital wave, going into the digital-to-analog converter.

SATB is an abbreviation for the four voice parts in any choir: soprano, alto, tenor, and bass. Each voice part sings in a different vocal range.

Saturation is a soft-clipping effect that adds roundness to tracks that need it, and excites particular harmonics in the sound. Saturation can be used for a rather specific purpose in sound engineering (such as rounding out the high-end) and for something as simple as adding a little warmth on the master bus. In some manner, saturation has characteristics of compression and limiting. Transient peaks usually get cut off, and the overall dynamic range decreases when saturation is used.

Tape Saturation Plugins are trying to recreate the sound of an audio signal being passed through tape hardware.

Tube Saturation Plugins are trying to recreate the sound of an audio signal being passed through tube hardware.

Scratching is a turntable mix technique, which involves moving the record back and forth by hand, creating different rhythmic sounds.

Scrubbing is the action of moving a piece of recorded audio back and forward, while monitoring it, generally to locate a particular point in the recording. Previously, scrubbing was performed with reel-to-reel analog tape, by manually turning the reels to pull the tape across the playhead, but today, scrubbing is mainly done digitally on a DAW, by moving the cursor back and forward across the waveform.

SCSI (Small Computer Systems Interface) is a high-speed communications protocol that allows computers, samplers, and disk drives to communicate with one another.

Segmented Meter is a series of LEDs, designed to indicate a level, such as audio level, by progressively displaying more LEDs as the level increases.

Semitone is a half of a tone and the minimum unit for measuring a musical interval. A semitone can be described as the closest distance between two sounds (in piano, this is the distance between two adjacent keys).

Sequence is the more or less exact repetition of a melody at a higher or lower pitch. If the repetition is only in the melody, with changed harmony, it is called a **melodic sequence**, and if the repetition is followed also in the harmony, a **harmonic sequence**; if, in order to preserve the exact intervals, the key is changed, it is called a **real sequence**; if the repetition is made without leaving the original key, which necessarily means that some of the intervals become larger or smaller by a semitone, it is called a **tonal sequence**;

sequences that are real in some repetitions and tonal in others are called **mixed sequences**.

Sequencer is a computerized device or software that can save, record, play, and edit audio files. The audio information can be stored in different data formats, such as MIDI, CV/G or OSC. Also, music sequencer can be introduced as a plugin with musical instruments or as a standalone unit.

Set (or "DJ Set") is a list of songs, which DJ plays during a performance.

Sharp means higher in pitch of the specific note by one semitone (half step).

Sibilance is a sound, characterized by the pronouncing of consonants, syllables, or words with the letter "s" (and sometimes "t" or "z"). It frequently refers to vocals and other aspects of music.

Sidechain is an auxiliary input to a signal processor that allows control of the processing to be triggered, by an external source. **Sidechaining** is a production technique used in a wide variety of music genres where an effect is activated by an audio track. In other words, it's using an alternative audio source to trigger a processor. The alternative source is set to a threshold, which when exceeded activates the effect.

Signal, in audio, is an alternating current (or voltage) matching the waveform, of being initially obtained from a sound pressure wave.

Signal-to-Noise Ratio (SNR) is a comparison of the strength of the signal level with the degree of noise, emitted by a device (expressed in dB).

Slipmat is a felt-type material used to reduce friction between the turntables plate and the vinyl.

Snake is a bunch of wires that carries audio signals. Snakes come in various types and configurations and are, primarily, used to route signals over long distances. The general usage for a snake is with the live sound systems. Microphone snake is used to connect all the stage mics to the mixing console. A snake makes connecting of microphones and different audio devices connecting more comfortable (and safer), because now you have a single multi-conductor cable, unlike many individual wires.

Song Position Pointer (SPP) is a MIDI message that allows connected MIDI devices to find a given point in the song. SPP used in conjunction with MIDI clock, as a way of synchronizing devices. An SPP message is usually sent in combination with a continue message, to start playback from the middle of a song.

Sound is a vibration that spreads like a normally audible mechanical wave of pressure and displacement, through a transmission medium, like air or water.

Sound Intensity (or "Acoustic Intensity") means a power carried by sound waves per unit area.

Sound types:

Acid Sound is a sound of the already vintage synthesizer that was actively used in electronic dance music of the 1990s (Roland TB-303).

Bright Sound is a sound with a lot of high frequencies.

Cold Sound means a sound with a plenty of high frequencies. It is the opposite of warm sound.

Direct Sound is the sound that reaches a microphone or a listener's ear without bouncing off any obstacles (as opposed to ambient or reflected sound).

Dry Sound is a definition that refers to sound without any processing or an effect (delay, reverb, etc.). Dry sound is the opposite of wet sound.

Hypersonic Sound (HSS) is a term used to describe the process, by which audible sound waves can be produced using ultrasonic sound waves that are free from non-linearity.

Impact Sound is a sound, produced by the collision of two solid objects.

Incident Sound means a sound that received directly from the source, i.e., first arriving sound without reflections.

Lead means any sound that might become the leading sound of your track.

Lush refers to a sound that is rich and full, almost to the point of excess.

Muddy is a term that means a very "muddy" sound (like there is no separation between vocals and instruments, between treble and bass frequencies, etc.).

Pads are any sounds that have the purpose of filling the mids and low mids of your track.

Reflected Sound is a sound that reaches a microphone or listener after one or more reflections from surrounding surfaces.

Sub-bass Sound is a sound with very low frequency (<60 Hz).

Ultrasound (or "Ultrasonic sound") is sound waves with frequencies above the upper audible limit of human hearing (higher 20,000 HZ).

Warm Sound is a sound with a lot of low mid/upper bass frequencies.

Wet Sound means a sound with effects, applied to it. The effects are usually added while recording, or while the sound is being "mixed."

Soundcheck is the process of setting up sound equipment and checking the sound before the concert starts.

Sound Design is the process of creating the sound effects, generally for a TV, Films, and Games.

Sound Diffusers interrupt discrete echoes, by diffusing sound energy over a broad area, without removing it from the room. This preserves the clarity of the sound and improves the intelligibility of speech.

Sound Engineer ("Audio Engineer" or "Sound Manager") is working on the technical aspects of audio and music production by mixing, producing, and managing the electronic effects of sound. Also, the term "sound engineer" is applied to the person, who uses a "Sound Desk" to mix signals that coming from a group on stage, or during a studio recording.

Sound Pressure Level (SPL) means the measure of the change in air pressure, produced by a sound wave (measured in dB). We hear and perceive SPL regarding the amplitude, volume, or loudness of the sound.

Sound Recording means the re-creation of sound waves. The sound that we hear around us is due to compression and rarefaction of the air; it is frequently necessary to convert these sound waves into electrical forms, so as to perform any modifications. Electric or mechanical capture of sound waves, such as voice, music or other sound effects, gives a meaning of audio recording.

Sound Synthesis is a method of creating sound from scratch, using electronic hardware or software.

Most common synthesis methods:

Additive Synthesis focuses on creating sound "from scratch," summing up sine wave partials at their corresponding amplitudes, until the desired timbre is reached.

Distortion Synthesis modifies existing sounds to produce more complex sounds (or timbres), normally by using non-linear circuits or mathematics. While some synthesis techniques achieve sonic complexity by using many oscillators, distortion methods produce a frequency spectrum that has many more components than oscillators.

Frequency Modulation Synthesis (FM Synthesis) is a method of sound synthesis, in which the frequencies are changed by the output of one or several additional oscillators to create a diversity of harmonically rich sounds.

Granular Synthesis is a basic sound synthesis technique that operates on the microsound time scale. The sound can be broken down into very slight fragments and combined to create different timbres and, consequently, very complex harmonically structured waveforms.

Linear Arithmetic Synthesis (LA Synthesis) is a form of synthesis that based on the sum of various sound elements, but with an approach fundamentally different to additive synthesis. The engineers, who created this type of synthesis, came up with the idea of using subtractive synthesis to produce the signal waveform and adding to it sampled sounds for the attack, while at the same time supplementing the primary waveform. Thanks to this trick, it was possible to get realistic-sounding attacks (which are a crucial element to identify a sound), while still enjoying the variation and "production" flexibility, provided by subtractive synthesis.

Phase Distortion Synthesis works by reading out a sinusoidal table that stored in memory. The most significant bits of the initial linear frequency counter, under envelope control, transformed into a secondary phase angle signal. This signal reads the sine wave.

Depending on the wiring, the conversion will change with a possible wide variety of wave shapes.

Physical Modeling Synthesis uses set algorithms to define the harmonic and acoustic characteristics of the generated sound. This method is often used to create real sounding instruments, as it is programmed to make particular distinctions between different aspects of the instrument.

Sample-based Synthesis is a type of audio synthesis that employs sampled sounds or instruments as the foundation for its sounds. The advantage of this method is the relatively small computational power required, as the tonal characteristics of each instrument are "built in" in the samples.

Subtractive Synthesis is a sound synthesis method, in which sounds are created by generating harmonically rich waveforms and then filtering out unwanted harmonics, to achieve the desired sound.

Vector Synthesis is a synthesis method, in which four user-selectable waveforms are mixed, using a quad panner before the result is sent to a filter or other processing.

Wavetable Synthesis is, perhaps, the oldest technique for creating sounds with computers. This method employs the use of a table with different switchable frequencies, played in certain orders (wavetables). Wavetable synthesis stores digital sound samples from various instruments, which can then be combined, edited and improved to reproduce the sound, defined by the digital input signal. This method was designed to create digital sound noises.

Sound Wave (or "Sound Pressure Wave") is a wave caused by a vibration that results in insignificant variations in air pressure, which we hear as a sound. The vibration disturbs the particles in the surrounding medium; then those particles bother particles next to them and so on. It creates a movement in wave pattern, just like waves in the ocean. The wave carries the sound energy through the medium, generally in all directions, and less intensely as it moves farther from the source. For sound engineers and music producers, it is very important to know the main sound waveforms.

Waveform is a visual representation or graphic of a sound wave, audio signal, or another type of wave, showing the wave's oscillations below and above the zero line.

Wave Number is the number of waves that exist over a specified distance.

There are five major waveforms:

Sine Wave (or "Sinusoidal wave") is the purest wave that contains only the fundamental frequency. A sine wave can be considered the most fundamental building block of sound.

Square Wave is a waveform that quickly rises to a particular level, remains constant for some period, then instantly drops to another level and stays there, and finally, rises to its original level to complete the wave cycle. The square wave differs from the sinusoidal wave in that besides the fundamental frequency it also contains odd harmonics. This waveform has a rich and pretty "raspy" sound.

Sawtooth Wave is a waveform that rises from a zero value to a peak value and then quickly drops to a zero value, for each cycle.

The result looks like the teeth of a saw (hence the name). Sawtooth wave contains a significant amount of even harmonics, unlike many of the other waveforms, produced by common VCOs. The result is bright, loud and "brassy" sound.

Pulse Wave is obtained directly from the square wave. It's a wave where absolute silence replaces the second part of the cycle. Pulse waves are not characterized by any frequency because there is only wave.

Triangle Wave sounds like something between a sine wave and a square wave. Just like a square wave, it contains the odd harmonics of the fundamental frequency, but the power of harmonics in the triangle wave is twice as low as their analogs in the square wave.

Space Music is a tranquil, hypnotic and moving music, which evokes a sense of deep listening and sensations of floating or flying.

Spectrum is the distribution of frequencies in any given sound.

Spill ("Bleed" or "Leakage") is a term, applied to acoustic interference from unwanted sound sources and sounds from other instruments that were not intended for recording.

Spinback means to spin the disc backward, to finish mix with a flourish.

Stab is a short sound used as a sample, normally for scratching.

Stems are isolated multi-tracks, typically bass, drums, vocals, guitar, keyboards, strings, etc., that make up a full song. If you want to sample or remix a song, having access to the stems gives you a highly greater flexibility: you can take a bass part or keyboard riff in isolation and combine it with other elements of the same song, or with parts of different songs, or with your own sounds, or all of the above. Also, a stem can mean a bounce of a group of tracks, usually with effects processing included.

Step Mode is a setting in a sequencer or DAW, in which notes are input manually, one note or step at a time.

Stereo is the reproduction of sounds, using two or more separate audio channels.

Stereo Image is an audible perception of a stereo signal, in which sources of different sounds appear to be coming from the far left, far right, or any place in between.

Sturdy means solid, powerful, and robust sound.

Stuttering (or "Glitch") is a vocal effect, achieved by chopping audio into slight sections, and then repeatedly copying and pasting them into the track.

Stylus is the part of a turntable's arm that makes contact with the vinyl being played.

Subcode means the additional information bits that are recorded alongside digital audio; used for playback and control purposes.

Submaster is a fader that controls the combined level of sound from several channels, during the recording or mixdown.

Submix is a mixing of tracks down to "stems," or sending them to group buses.

Sum is a signal that is the mix of two stereo channels at equal level and in phase. **Summing** is the process of mixing two or more signals down to a single mono or stereo output.

Surround Sound refers to a type of audio output, in which the sound appears to "surround the audience" by 360 degrees.

Syncopation is a deliberate upsetting of the compositions pulse through a temporary shifting of the accent to a weak beat or an off-beat, which leads to a violation of the listener's expectations, and the awakening of the desire to restore metric normality.

Synth (or "Synthesizer") is the musical instrument that generates its own sounds.

System Exclusive (SysEx) is a MIDI message that will only be recognized by a unit of a certain manufacturer.

Tachometer (or simple "Tach") is a device on the recorder that measures and regulates tape speed.

Tech House is a subgenre of house music that mixes elements of techno with house music. Tech house uses the same basic structure as house. However, some classic house elements are replaced with elements from techno such as shorter, deeper, darker and often distorted kicks, smaller, quicker hi-hats, noisier snares and more acid sounding synth melodies.

Techno is an EDM genre that emerged in Detroit, USA, during the mid-to-late 1980s. Stylistically, techno is repetitive instrumental music, characterized by artificial sound with an emphasis on mechanical rhythms. Tempo varies between 120 to 150 bpm, depending on the style of techno.

Tempo is the rate, at which the music moves; measured in beats per minute (BPM).

Most common tempos:

Larghissimo — very, very slow (20 bpm and below);
Grave — slow (20–40 bpm);

Lento — slowly (40–60 bpm);

Largo — broadly (40–60 bpm);

Larghetto — rather broadly (60–66 bpm);

Adagio — slow and stately, literally, "at ease" (66–76 bpm);

Adagietto — rather slow (70–80 bpm);

Andante Moderato — a bit slower than andante;

Andante — at a walking pace (76–108 bpm);

Andantino – slightly faster than andante;

Moderato — moderately (108–120 bpm);

Allegretto — moderately fast, but less so than allegro;

Allegro Moderato — moderately quick (112–124 bpm);

Allegro — fast, quickly and bright (120–168 bpm);

Vivace — lively and speedy, faster than allegro (140 bpm);

Vivacissimo — very fast and lively;

Allegrissimo — very quickly;

Presto — very fast (168–200 bpm);

Prestissimo — extremely fast (more than 200bpm).

Tempo Mapping is the act of setting a sequencer or DAW to track changes in the tempo of the recorded performance. Unlike beat mapping (which effectively adjust the recording to fit a set rate), tempo mapping regulates the tempo of the project (mainly the MIDI instruments) to match the original tempo nuances of the recorded material.

Threshold is a point, at which compression (or any other dynamic signal processing) begins.

Timbre is a sound quality that helps you to distinguish one instrument or voice from another, even when both instruments perform the same pitch.

Time Compression ("Time Stretching" or "Time Shifting") is the process of accelerating or slowing down an audio recording, without changing a pitch of the sounds.

Toms are the small drums (as little as 10-inch diameter), which mount on racks above the kick drum and the big drums in a drum set.

Tone can mean:
1) Any single-frequency signal or sound;
2) One of the several single-frequency signals at the beginning of a tape reel at the magnetic reference level, which will be used to record the program;
3) The sound quality of an instrument's sound about the amount of energy, present at various frequencies;

4) In some synthesizers, this term means an audio signal, similar to the sound of the instrument that will be put out by the unit.

Trance is an EDM genre that developed during the 1990s in Germany. Tracks in this style are often characterized by a soothing effect and can also act as a hymn. The composition in this style usually consists of a short repeating melody, a bass line, and a simple percussion part (the bass drum sounds for every beat of the beat); tempo lying between 125 - 150 BPM.

Transient is a high-amplitude, short-duration oscillation of a sudden impulse that appears at the beginning of a sound.

Transient Shaper is a small version of the compressor, created to work with the timing parameters of the signal (Attack and Release). A typical transient shaper allows you to change the amplitude and increase the level of attack, and restore the signal, according to the chosen curve.

Transitions are the sounds, riffs, or rhythmic sections that connect adjacent musical sections together.

Transpose mean to shift a set of musical notes by a fixed interval. For example, one might transpose an entire piece of music into another key. Similarly, one might transpose a tone row or a chord so that it begins on another pitch.

Trap is a music genre, which originated in the 1990s in the United States. Trap music employs a widely use of multi-layered, hard-lined, and melodic synthesizer; deep kick drums; powerful high-hats, accelerated in two, three or more times. Trap music is defined by its ominous, bleak and gritty lyrics, which often include observation of hardship, violence, street life, poverty, and harsh experiences in urban surroundings. The tempo of trap beat is around 140 BPM.

Treble means the upper part of the frequency range, which is controllable by DJ mixers. This range, generally, contains hi-hats, shakers, and some parts of voices.

Tremolo is a wavering or "shaking" sound effect created either by quick repetitions of the notes (as in a violin tremolo) or by quick changes in amplitude.

Tri-amping is the practice of connecting three channels of amplification to a loudspeaker unit: one to power the bass driver (woofer), one to power the mid-range and the third to power the treble driver (tweeter).

Trigger is a signal (or the action of sending a signal), which represents the appearance of an event (such as a key press) with a brief pulse, after which the signal returns to its base state. In drumming, the trigger is an electronic transducer that can be affixed to a drum, cymbal or another instrument to allow it to control an electronic drum unit or similar device.

Trim Control is a device that reduces or increases the signal strength in amplifier, often over a limited range.

Tropical House is a subgenre of deep house, which possesses typical house music characteristics, but has more uplifting and relaxing sound. The tempo of tropical house songs varies between 110 and 115 BPM.

Truncation can mean:
1) The shortening of an audio signal, song or sample, generally by cutting off the end;
2) The dropping of data bits, when the bit resolution is reduced (for example, from 24-bit to 16-bit), creating digital distortion.

Turntable can mean:
1) One of two round disc platters, located on a tape machine, that holds the tape

reels in place, sometimes with a locking mechanism;
2) A device that used to playback a phonograph record, consisting of a disc or platter, rotated by a motor, and a tonearm that contains a stylus and cartridge.

Turntablism is the art of creating sounds and music, by manipulating turntables and a DJ mixer. The person performing this kind of art is called a "turntablist."

Tweeter can mean:
1) A speaker that designed to reproduce only the high frequencies of the sound;
2) The driver in a loudspeaker cabinet, created to produce the higher range of audio frequencies, generally from about 1,000 Hz up to around 20 kHz (also called a "high-frequency drive").

Two-way Speaker is a speaker system with separate speakers, to reproduce the lower frequencies (woofer) and the higher frequencies (tweeter).

Ultraharmonic Response describes frequencies that are not whole number multipliers but fractional multiples of the fundamental frequency of the system, e.g. 1.5 or 2.5 times the fundamental frequency.

Unison is a term that refers to several performers, instruments, or sound sources that are sounding at the same time and with the equivalent pitch.

Vamp is a repeating musical section or accompaniment used in different music genres. A vamp may consist of a single chord or a sequence of chords played in a repeated rhythm.

Vamp and Fade is a method of ending the recording of a song, in which the music has a repeating part, and the sound engineer or producer reduces volume until the music fades out.

VBR (Variable Bitrate) is a variant of data encoding, in which the bit rate can vary from one fragment of the file to another, depending on the saturation of the audio material.

VCA (Voltage-Controlled Amplifier) is a device that responds to any change in voltage at its control input, by altering the amplification of a signal being passed through it. Most VCAs could be more accurately called **Voltage-Controlled Attenuators** as they reduce the signal level (depending on the input CV), but they don't usually amplify it.

VCO (Voltage-Controlled Oscillator) is an oscillator, whose frequency can be changed by altering the amount of voltage being sent to its control input.

Velocity is a measure of how quickly and powerfully a key on a keyboard is pressed, when the player initially presses the key.

Verse is the first main section of your melody; it repeats a few times before moving into the chorus. Verses are, typically, used in music with lyrics.

Vibration is a periodic oscillation of an object when it's displaced from the rest position or position of equilibrium (as in transmitting sound).

Vibration Dose is a parameter that combines the magnitude of vibration and the time for which it occurs.

Vibrato means a smooth and repeated changing of the pitch up and down from the regular musical pitch.

Vocal Booth is an isolation room used for vocal recording. A vocal booth should generally have a dry sound. The walls and ceiling are covered with absorbers to prevent any reflections from reaching the microphone.

Vocoder is an audio processing device or plug-in that analyzes the features of an audio signal and uses them to influence another synthesized signal. The vocoder is used, mainly, for producing synthesized voice effects from human speech (it creates the characteristic robotic vocal).

Volume Unit (VU) is a unit to measure perceived loudness changes in audio.

Vox is a Latin word that means "voice"; frequently used as an abbreviation for track logs in the studio.

VST (Virtual Studio Technology) is the most known interface for integrating audio synths and effects plugins with your DAW.

VST3 is an update to the VST plug-in standard that offered completely rewritten code with a lot of new features.

Walking Bass Line is a series of notes, played to lead the song from one chord to another.

WAV (Waveform Audio File Format) is the primary audio file format, used on Windows systems for raw and, typically, uncompressed audio.

Wavelength means the physical length of one cycle of a wave; the longer the wavelength of a sound wave, the lower its frequency; the shorter the wavelength, the higher its frequency.

Weighting is an equalization curve used in audio tests that compensates for the Fletcher-Munson Curve at various levels.

Whole Step is a change in pitch equivalent to two half steps, or the difference in pitch between two piano keys.

Windscreen is a device that reduces or eliminates wind noise, for example from the microphone being moved, etc.

Witch House is a dark electronic music genre that emerged in the early 2010s.

The music in this genre is heavily influenced by chopped and screwed hip-hop soundscapes, industrial and noise experimentation, and features use of drum machines, synthesizers, dark samples, droning repetition, and profoundly altered, ethereal, indiscernible vocals.

Woofer can mean:
1) A speaker created to reproduce only bass frequencies;
2) A part of a speaker system designed to handle the low-frequency parts of the signal;
3) A drive unit, operating only in the bass frequencies.

XLR (Xtended Locking Round) is a type of connector, usually having three pins, which is used with balanced audio connections.

Y- Cord (Y Connector) is a cable with three connectors so that one output may be sent to two inputs.

Zero Crossing is a point, at which a digitally encoded waveform crosses the center of its amplitude range.

ZOH (Zero-Order Hold) refers to the mathematical expression of the signal processing, done by a conventional D/A converter.

Made in the USA
Middletown, DE
31 July 2020